Joan Hustace Walker

Great Pyrenees

Everything about Purchase, Care, Nutrition, Behavior, and Training

Filled with full-color photographs

Illustrations by
Michele Earle-Bridges

BARRON'S

2 CONTENTS

HISTORY OF THE GREAT PYRENEES

One look at a Great Pyrenees, and even the most casual observer can't resist becoming an ardent admirer of the breed. Though difficult to pinpoint, there is something incredibly compelling in this dog's distant and almost aloof gaze. The breed's unique, almond-shaped eyes are striking, and its thick, dense white coat complements the dog's large, strong body. Without a doubt, the Great Pyrenees is a commanding animal of breathtaking beauty.

Le Chien de Montagne Pyrénées

The breed has its origins in the southwest of France and the northeast of Spain in the circle of mountains and surrounding valleys inhabited by the Basque people. The Great Pyrenees, known in France as *Le Chien de Montagne Pyrénées* (the dog of the Pyrenees Mountain), initially served as a livestock guardian.

The great white dogs were bred centuries ago to be not only beautiful, but functional as well. The dog's coarse, long white coat was

The Great Pyrenees is a working breed, and is as much at home on a farm as in a suburban home.

resilient to unpredictable mountain weather. Its light coloration enabled the dog to blend in easily with the sheep, which were also predominantly white. The Pyr's calm temperament soothed the sheep. Its alert nocturnal nature coupled with a keen sense of vision, hearing, and scent made it difficult for any would-be predator to escape detection, and its large size, strength, and courage enabled it to fight wolves and bears with unparalleled ferocity. And, of course, the breed's intelligence allowed it to work solo, without the guidance or supervision of its owner, who very well might be sound asleep in a mountainside shepherd's hut.

The specialized abilities of the Great Pyrenees were essential to the livelihood of the largely secluded Basque people who depended heavily on the safety and welfare of their sheep. For centuries, and in some areas today, Basque shepherds would take their flocks up into the rich mountain pastures to graze during warmer months, and then later return to lower pastures when heavy snows threatened. During these summers in the mountains, the shepherds formed a sort of pastoral syndicate and lived in communal huts, tending to their flocks and making cheese from sheep's milk.

Early Duties

As a pastoral guardian, the role of the Great Pyrenees with the Basque shepherds was not as a herding dog. The actual herding tasks were relegated to a small, tireless breed called the Pyrenean Shepherd or Le Petit Berger. The Great Pyrenees' duty was to protect sheep from hungry wild bear and wolf attacks. And, if there is any truth to ancient Basque folklore, the Great Pyrenees also may have defended its charges from the legendary (and at one time greatly feared) "hairy god of the forest."

Interestingly, the pairing of a large white dog breed with a smaller herding dog is not an uncommon sight in Europe. In Italy there is the Maremma and its little companion the Bergamese Shepherd. The Kuvasz is Hungary's pastoral guard and the Puli is its shepherd. In Poland, the Tatra Mountain Dog was developed to guard flocks and the Valee or Nizinny Shepherd served as the herder.

Origin

The most current theory as to the origin of the Great Pyrenees (and other breeds like it) is that many of the livestock protection dogs originated from Asia Minor and were brought to Europe by both land (with Aryan hordes) and by sea (with Phoenician traders into Spain). Other researchers propose that as trade of livestock, grain, spices, silks, and gold moved along the Silk Road from the Middle East, India, and China to Europe, livestock guardian dogs moved along this path, too. And, pups that were whelped along the way may have been sold or left with shepherds along the route.

Regardless of the breed's ultimate origin, the Great Pyrenees is one of the oldest breeds alive today and much is known about its colorful and well-known past in France.

Beyond a Livestock Guardian Dog

Though the Basque historically have developed an isolated culture and even today speak a language that is distinct and unrelated to either Spanish or French, the secret of their fabulous working dog eventually moved beyond the seclusion of their rich mountain pastures. Word of the Great Pyrenees' tremendous guarding abilities quickly spread into adjoining regions.

In the Middle Ages, the lords and landowners of the Pyrenean region began seeking out Great Pyrenees for use as trained guard and attack dogs. While working sentry duty for the immense mountainside châteaux in Foix, Lourdes, and Carcassonne, the dogs were reportedly trained to hunt down and attack highwaymen, cattle thieves, or other ne'er-do-wells. There was a time during the 1400s when many of these great châteaux boasted of having a band of Great Pyrenees as protection.

The great white dog also was, for a short while, the darling of a few members of French royalty. According to one account, in 1675, the son of Louis XIV was in Barrèges, France, visiting the countryside when he discovered a young, male Pyrenees named Patou (shepherd). Totally taken by the dog, the young boy brought the dog home to live with him at the Louvre in Paris.

Soon after, the Marquis de Louvois reportedly traveled specifically to the Pyrenean region to acquire a prized male, which he brought back to the Palace of Versailles—where the dog immediately became a court favorite.

By the 1800s the Great Pyrenees was gaining in popularity across Europe and England; however, it would take more than 100 years before the breed would become popular in the United States—as both a show dog and working dog.

Beginnings of a Show Dog

In the mid-1800s Britain's Queen Victoria owned one of the great white dogs. In 1885 the Kennel Club in London recognized the "Pyrenean Mountain Dog" in its registry. Soon after this recognition, the first dogs representing the breed were shown at the Crystal Palace in London. The Great Pyrenees, however, was not bred in England on a regular basis until 1935, when Jeanne Harper Trois Fontaines founded the De Fontenay kennel. Her breeding was to become world renowned.

Meanwhile, in the homeland of the Great Pyrenees, the breed was becoming rare. As wolves and bears became scarcer and scarcer, the threat to the flocks was gradually removed, and the raison d'être for a pastoral guardian dog was no longer required.

In order to help preserve what was left of the breed, two breed clubs were formed in 1907, and breed standards that described the ideal Pyr were written; however, the clubs were unable to settle their differences. Though vigilant efforts were made to reestablish the breed, the clubs, in their disunity, lacked strength.

During World War I, breed historians say that the Great Pyrenees was used for pack service and liaison work. The breed may even have been called upon to carry contraband goods across the Franco-Spanish border, since it was capable of traversing treacherous mountain paths through the Pyrenees mountains.

World War I also brought a time of great tribulation for the breed and its owners. The two breed clubs that had been formed in France were disbanded; many of the region's prominent kennels were no more. Often, the lack of food forced tearful breeders and owners to euthanize their prized Pyrenees. Those dogs able to survive did so—just barely. At the end of the war, it was recorded that the malnourished surviving dogs were often unable to breed. The postwar registry included only 20 registrations in 10 years—all without pedigrees.

To change this sad state of affairs for the Great Pyrenees, the Réunion des Amateurs de Chiens Pyrénéens (RACP) was formed by Frenchman Bernard Senac-Lagrange, along with several dedicated breeders. From 1920 to 1930 Senac-Lagrange is credited with accomplishing more for the breed in ten years than had been accomplished by others in centuries. The club combined not only Pyrenees fanciers, but also those involved with the breed's coworker, the Petit Berger, as well as other Pyrenean breeds. The club grew to more than 100 members, and in 1927 a new Great Pyrenees breed standard was published, which served as the basis for today's standard. (See page 8.)

Travel to America

The true salvation of the breed came about in 1930, when Francis and Mary Crane in Needham, Massachusetts, fell in love with two adorable, snow-white puppies from France and began a breeding program in 1931. If it had not been for the Cranes' involvement in the breed, many owners believe the breed would be extinct. They exhibited their dogs with great success all over the United States, always taking time to talk to new breeders and owners to help promote the breed. The Cranes are credited with helping the breed survive the ravages of World War II. During the war years, the

Cranes' Basquaerie kennel maintained more than 100 Pyrs, many from the finest breeders in France.

In 1933 the American Kennel Club (AKC) recognized the Great Pyrenees as a breed. The following year, the Great Pyrenees Club of America (GPCA) was organized, and in 1935 the GPCA became a member breed club of the AKC. The breed's original standard, which was adopted from the French standard drafted in 1927, was revised in 1935 and remained unchanged until 1990.

These Pyrs demonstrate the qualities of elegance and majesty described in the breed standard.

Official Standard for the Great Pyrenees

General Appearance–The Great Pyrenees dog conveys the distinct impression of elegance and unsurpassed beauty combined with great overall size and majesty. He has a white or prin-

"Captein Berry," a nineteenth century oil painting by French artist Charles Boland.

cipally white coat that may contain markings of badger, gray, or varying shades of tan. He possesses a keen intelligence and a kindly, while regal, expression. Exhibiting a unique elegance of bearing and movement, his soundness and coordination show unmistakably the purpose for which he has been bred: The strenuous work of guarding the flocks in all kinds of weather on the steep mountain slopes of the Pyrenees.

Size, Proportion, Substance

Size—The height at the withers ranges from 27 inches to 32 inches for dogs and from 25 inches to 29 inches for bitches. A 27-inch dog weighs about 100 pounds and a 25-inch bitch weighs about 85 pounds. Weight is in proportion to the overall size and structure. *Proportion*—The Great Pyrenees is a balanced dog with the height measured at the withers being somewhat less than the length of the body measured from the point of the shoulder to the rearmost projection of the upper thigh (buttocks). These proportions create a somewhat rectangular dog, slightly longer than it is tall. Front and rear angulation are balanced. *Substance*—The Great Pyrenees is a dog of medium substance whose coat deceives those who do not feel the bone and muscle. Commensurate with his size and impression of elegance there is sufficient bone and muscle to provide a balance with the frame. *Faults*—Size: Dogs and bitches under minimum size or over maximum size. Substance: Dogs too heavily boned or too lightly boned to be in balance with their frame.

Head—Correct head and expression are essential to the breed. The head is not heavy in proportion to the size of the dog. It is wedge shaped with a slightly rounded crown. *Expression*—The expression is elegant, intelligent and contemplative. *Eyes*—Medium sized, almond shaped, set slightly obliquely, rich dark brown. Eyelids are close fitting with black rims. *Ears*—Small to medium in size, V-shaped with rounded tips, set on at eye level, normally carried low, flat and close to the head. There is a characteristic meeting of the hair of the upper and lower face which forms a line from the outer corner of the eye to the base of the ear. *Skull and Muzzle*—The muzzle is approximately equal in length to the back skull. The width and length of the skull are approximately equal. The muzzle blends smoothly with the skull. The cheeks are flat. There is sufficient fill under the eyes. A slight furrow exists between the eyes. There is no apparent stop. The bony eyebrow ridges are only slightly developed. Lips are tight fitting with the upper lip just covering the lower lip. There is a strong lower jaw. The nose and lips are black. *Teeth*—A scissors bite is preferred, but a level bite is acceptable. It is not unusual to see dropped (receding) lower central incisor teeth. *Faults*—Too heavy head (St. Bernard or Newfoundland-like). Too narrow or small skull. Foxy appearance. Presence of an apparent stop. Missing pigmentation on nose, eye rims, or lips. Eyelids round, triangular, loose or small. Overshot, undershot, wry mouth.

Neck, Topline, Body

Neck—Strongly muscled and of medium length, with minimal dewlap. *Topline*—The backline is level. *Body*—The chest is moderately broad. The rib cage is well sprung, oval in shape, and of sufficient depth to reach the elbows. Back and loin are broad and strongly coupled with some tuck-up. The croup is gently sloping with the tail set on just below the level of the back. *Tail*—The tail bones are of sufficient length to reach the hock. The tail is well plumed, carried low in repose and may be carried over the back, "making the wheel," when aroused. When present, a "shepherd's crook" at the end of the tail accentuates the plume. When gaiting, the tail may be carried either over the back or low. Both carriages are equally correct. *Fault*—Barrel ribs.

Forequarters

Shoulders—The shoulders are well laid back, well muscled and lie close to the body. The upper arm meets the shoulder blade at approximately a right angle. The upper arm angles backward from the point of the shoulder to the elbow and is never perpendicular to the ground. The length of the shoulder blade and the upper arm is approximately equal. The height from the ground to the elbow appears approximately equal to the height from the elbow to the withers. *Forelegs*—The legs are of sufficient bone and muscle to provide a balance with the frame. The elbows are close to the body and point directly to the rear when standing and gaiting. The forelegs, when viewed from the side, are located directly under the withers and are straight and vertical to the ground. The elbows, when viewed from the front, are set in a straight line from the point of shoulder to the wrist. Front pasterns are strong and flexible. Each foreleg carries a single dewclaw. *Front Feet*—Rounded, close-cupped, well padded, toes well arched.

Hindquarters—The angulation of the hindquarters is similar in degree to that of the forequarters. *Thighs*—Strongly muscular upper thighs extend from the pelvis at right angles. The upper thigh is the same length as the lower thigh, creating moderate stifle joint angulation when viewed in profile. The rear pastern (metatarsus) is of medium length and perpendicular to the ground as the dog stands naturally. This produces a moderate degree of angulation in the hock joint, when viewed from the side. The hindquarters from the hip to the rear pastern are straight and parallel, as viewed from the rear. The rear legs are of sufficient bone and muscle to provide a balance with the frame. Double dewclaws are located on each rear leg. *Rear Feet*—The rear feet have a structural tendency to toe out slightly. This breed characteristic is not to be confused with cow-hocks. The rear feet, like the forefeet, are rounded, close-cupped, well padded, with toes well arched. *Fault*—Absence of double dewclaws on each rear leg.

Coat—The weather resistant double coat consists of a long, flat, thick outer coat of coarse hair, straight or slightly undulating, and lying over a dense, fine, woolly undercoat. The coat is more profuse about the neck and shoulders where it forms a ruff or mane which is more pronounced in males. Longer hair on the tail forms a plume. There is feathering along the back of the front legs and along the back of the thighs, giving a "pantaloon" effect. The hair on the face and ears is shorter and of finer texture. Correctness of coat is more important than abundance of coat. *Faults*—Curly coat. Stand-off coat (Samoyed type).

Color—White or white with markings of gray, badger, reddish brown, or varying shades of tan. Markings of varying size may appear on the ears, head (including a full face mask), tail and as a few body spots. The undercoat may be white or shaded. All of the above described colorings and location are characteristic of the breed and equally correct. *Fault*—Outer coat markings covering more than one third of the body.

Gait—The Great Pyrenees moves smoothly and elegantly, true and straight ahead, exhibiting both power and agility. The stride is well balanced with good reach and strong drive. The legs tend to move toward the center line as speed increases. Ease and efficiency of movement are more important than speed.

Temperament—Character and temperament are of utmost importance. In nature, the Great Pyrenees is confident, gentle, and affectionate. While territorial and protective of his flock or family when necessary, his general demeanor is one of quiet composure, both patient and tolerant. He is strong willed, independent and somewhat reserved, yet attentive, fearless and loyal to his charges both human and animal.

Although the Great Pyrenees may appear reserved in the show ring, any sign of excessive shyness, nervousness, or aggression to humans is unacceptable and must be considered an extremely serious fault.

Approved June 12, 1990
Effective August 1, 1990

UNDERSTANDING YOUR GREAT PYRENEES

If you think an adult Pyr is stunning, wait until you see a puppy. Sure, all puppies are cute, but Great Pyrenees puppies are irresistible. Fluffy and white or mostly white with dark eyes and black noses, a Pyrenees puppy will tug at the heartstrings of even the most stalwart dog owners. But, before you promise a puppy to your family (or to yourself!), you should carefully weigh the pros and cons of the breed, and then decide whether owning a Pyr is the right decision for you.

The Great Pyrenees is a dog bred for centuries to excel at certain tasks. Some of the behaviors required of this breed to perform its job translate well into life as a pet; other characteristics some owners may find challenging. It is important, therefore, when considering the Pyr as a pet for life, to have an understanding of characteristic Pyr behaviors and to understand how well these behaviors will fit into your lifestyle.

Attributes of the Pyr

Without a doubt, one of the greatest attractions of the Great Pyrenees is its magnificent beauty. The shape of the dog's eyes and head

Make sure you teach your child's friends and frequent visitors how to treat a dog nicely.

leave an unforgettable impression. The Pyr's double coat is also a quality that routinely evokes "oooohs" and "aaaahs" from ringside spectators. In addition to being beautiful, the coat is relatively carefree. If correct, a dry coat sheds dirt easily and requires only about 30 minutes of brushing each week. But of course, beauty is only skin deep—and even the most beautiful dog must have other redeeming qualities if it is to survive as a popular dog. The Pyr has many.

Health

For some breeds, health can be a major issue. In the Pyrenees, however, poor health is not usually a concern. For the most part, the Great Pyrenees is an exceptionally robust and healthy breed. With a well-bred dog that has been given an appropriately safe and nurturing environment that includes good sound nutrition and regular exercise, an owner can reasonably expect a Pyr to live a full and healthy life of 10 to 12 years.

Intelligence

The Great Pyrenees is also blessed with great intelligence and is alert but very calm in nature. This makes sense when one considers the dog's background. A hyperactive, always moving dog would not have had a calming effect on the sheep it was watching, nor would it have had the energy necessary for the occasional fight with wild animals. A calm dog, of course, translates into a wonderful house dog that is satisfied with daily exercise and perhaps a 20-minute evening patrol of the backyard fence—just to make sure everything is safe.

Guarding Ability

Even though only working Pyrs are required to perform guard duty, the pet Pyr still takes its guard work seriously—though in the home this translates to guarding family, home, and even small pets. The Great Pyrenees is a loving, staunchly devoted dog to its family. (Pyrs are not overly friendly to strangers and tend to keep a polite but watchful eye on any strangers to their home.)

Another admirable quality of the Great Pyrenees is its great strength and athletic ability. There are many activities, both competitive and noncompetitive, which the Pyr can perform well. The breed enjoys and is adept at pulling carts. It can be competitive in obedience and is a natural showstopper in the conformation ring. The breed's true forte, of course, is in guarding livestock. Though used mostly for guarding sheep during its long history in France, the breed also can be trained to guard other livestock, such as horses. The GPCA reports that Pyrs in the United States working as livestock guardians far outnumber the remaining working Pyrs in the breed's homeland, France.

Pet owners who are not using their Pyrs as livestock guardians will generally find that the breed's guarding instincts transpose to the dog's human family. In other words, in a home with a Pyr, it is highly unlikely that a stranger will reach your front door or even the bottom of your driveway without your Pyr sounding the alarm with a deep, throaty bark that certainly means business.

On another note, the Great Pyrenees' generations of guarding helpless animals seems to have translated into a propensity for guarding or at least tolerating smaller pets. The breed has a low prey drive and when raised with kittens, cats, rabbits, lambs, and so on, it frequently lives peaceably, side-by-side with these curious creatures. However, living with other large, "alpha" guardian-type dogs may produce some difficulties.

Challenges of the Breed

Dog–Dog Aggression

The Great Pyrenees was not bred to get along with other dogs. It was bred to guard livestock, keep the shepherd company, and tolerate that pesky little herding dog. It was also bred to scare off, or kill if it must, any threats to its charges. Centuries ago, that meant wolves and Pyrenean brown bears. Today, the Pyr is called upon to protect livestock in the United States from coyotes and wild dogs. This breed remains a ferocious fighter, so, no matter how sweet and gentle a Pyr is with its owners, it should never be considered a harmless, fluffy white dog.

Troubles can occur, say Pyr owners, when the dogs are asked to live with other large, dominant breeds, such as Rottweilers or Malamutes, that would challenge the Pyrenees for territory (see The Pyr as a Second Pet, page 51).

Two Pyrs may not be better than one. Male-male and female-female pairings may end up in destructive fighting, and put the owner in the position of either separating the dogs for eternity or getting rid of one or the other. If you fall in love with the breed and simply must have more than one, experienced breeders say the best pairings are generally male-female.

Temperament Challenges

The Great Pyrenees is *not* aggressive toward people. Aggressiveness toward people is considered a *serious flaw* in a dog and not tolerated by responsible breeders or owners. However, the Pyrenees can be dominating, and this trait, coupled with its size and keen intelligence, can be a challenge in the hands of an inexperienced, timid, or frail owner.

The Pyrenees' willful streak probably dates back centuries to its original task of guarding sheep: The Pyr had to be intelligent enough to discern trouble and independent enough to act on its own without waiting for the shepherd's command. In other words, the dog was required to make decisions.

To overcome an independent, self-sufficient streak or to make sure a Pyrenees never discovers it is capable of dominating anyone in a home, good socialization skills and consistent obedience training are an absolute must with this breed. A dog raised in isolation will *not* know how to behave around people. A dog of this size (some weigh more than 100 pounds [45 kg]) must be well trained and respect its owner. It also must be given the correct environment in which to develop into an even-tempered dog. Though temperament is largely inherited, many experts believe that a good environment reinforces good temperament, and a bad environment can tip a borderline temperament the wrong way.

So, Great Pyrenees *must be trained*. And their owners must not be timid or easily challenged.

Adolescence

Adolescence is the same for dogs as it is for humans. Adolescence means you have a fully grown dog with raging hormones (if it's not neutered), and a will for displaying independence. If your dog (particularly if it is a male) hits the 10- to 20-month-old "teenage years" without respect for its owner and a good, solid grounding in obedience, an owner might find himself or herself in a difficult situation.

Roaming

Because of the breed's guarding instincts, your Pyr should always be walked on a leash and safely restricted to a backyard with a sturdy, high fence. However, there is an additional reason why this breed should never be left off-leash or expected to sit in the front yard without a fence: The dog was bred to guard large territories.

According to Basque historians, a shepherd's flocks may have numbered more than 300. Also, the shepherds shared common grazing grounds and so the communal herd easily may have numbered more than 3,000 sheep and their lambs. The guard dogs were expected to guard a number of livestock in a large area.

So, if you're going to own a Pyr, build a fence for your yard and plan daily walks on a leash.

Invisible fences and Pyrs do not do well. Most Pyrs will endure the electric jolt to get out of the fence but will not consider getting shocked just to get back in. Even with a dog that doesn't leave the fence, if another animal or dog enters the Pyr's yard, it will probably not survive the Pyr's attack.

Shedding

The Pyr's luxuriant white coat is not only beautiful, but also an exquisite tactile experience. (Pyrenees hair is a preferred wool among some knitters and makes silky soft sweaters and warm outer garments.) The coat is considered wash and wear because mud, when dry, literally falls out of the coat. However, it is a full, dense, thick long coat—and the dogs *do* shed—particularly in the spring. Regular grooming is required, and though perhaps not as involved as other heavily coated breeds, it does require at least a weekly commitment, and that means *time* that some owners may not have. (In the spring, daily brushing is necessary as *buckets* of hair are shed at this time.)

The Great Pyrenees tends to be very tolerant of smaller, less dominant animals if introduced to them as a puppy.

Owning a long white-coated dog also means not being able to sit down in your home in a dark suit and stand up again without having white hairs where they shouldn't be. So if you're a neat freak, you are either going to have to increase your cleaning or lower your cleanliness standards, or consider signing up for therapy sessions *now*. Of course, if the beauty of the coat and the love of the dog far outweigh your aversion to occasional floating hair balls, then you should do just fine.

Night Barking

This is a biggy. The GPCA rescue committee (club members involved in placing unwanted adult Pyrs into loving homes) says that the most common complaint of people who are giving up their Pyrs is that the dogs barked a lot, especially at night. This is a critical characteristic of the Pyr that potential owners *must* understand and accept if they are to be successful as Pyr owners.

As a guard dog, a Pyr will bark if it hears *anything* suspicious. It could be a prowler. It could be a squirrel rustling in the shrubbery. It could even be the wind rustling the leaves in a tree. At any noise, the Pyr will give an alert bark. This bark means, "I heard something. It might

You'll want to plunge your hands into the Pyr's luxuriant coat.

be something I'm listening and trying to figure it out." If it's nothing, the dog becomes silent again. Of course, your dog may hear a new noise every few hours, or every few minutes.

If what the dog hears amounts to something "real," the barking will pick up and become more insistent and determined. The Pyr may be able to be trained to stop barking upon its owner's command—or it may not. With some Pyrenees, barking is not a big factor; with others, it can be major. Being nocturnal, some Pyrenees may seem to be up all night with on-again, off-again barking. Will this drive you crazy? Will it drive your neighbors crazy? In many instances, the answers have been "yes" to both.

There are other owners, however, who understand the reason for night barking (or appreciate the guardlike qualities of this dog) and either train their dog to stop barking on command, keep their dog indoors if in a suburban or urban setting, or simply tolerate the nightly interruptions. (For information on discouraging barking, see page 78.)

Destructiveness

Pyrs can be fence climbers. They also *love* to dig big holes in which to lie in the summertime. But these problems are usually worse when the dog is isolated from its family and bored. It is important to understand that although the breed worked for centuries in isolated areas, it was not isolated from the kind touch and affection of human companionship. One of its jobs as a working dog was to be a companion to the shepherds.

Today, the Pyr has an equally important need for receiving love and attention from its family. It enjoys being outside, but it prefers being outside with its owner. If its owner is inside, the Pyr would prefer to be inside, too. If the Pyr is left outside with no attention, expect potholes, chewed fencing and furniture, and ripped screens.

Life with a Large Dog

Size, depending on how you look at it, can be either an asset or a drawback. When it comes to the Great Pyrenees, let's hope you consider it an asset. A female Pyr is usually between 85 and 100 pounds (38.5 to 45 kg). A male Pyr can tip the scales at 120 pounds (54 kg) and measure more than 31 inches (79 cm) at the shoulder. If you've never owned a large dog before, there are a few facts of big dog life that you should be prepared for before committing yourself to a large dog.

Height

A Pyr can make a clean swipe of your kitchen counters without even standing up on two legs. The dog's tremendous sense of smell will swiftly locate any morsel of food accidentally left on the counter. Meat left to thaw on the counter may be gone by the time you get there. With a Pyr as a pet, if you can't keep your counters clear of food, then be sure to keep the telephone number of a local pizza delivery service in a handy place.

The Pyr's height and general size can also be intimidating to friends, visitors ("Oh my, what a *big* dog!"), and even family members. It's not unheard of for a parent to purchase a puppy, only to discover that the adult dog's size frightens the children. To avoid making this mistake, be sure you recognize just how large this breed is. Their appearance in the park may seem fine, but when a 100-plus-pound (45-plus-kg) dog comes trotting into your living room, your impression may be quite different. *Visit with a breeder and his or her adult dogs* to get an idea of how big is big. See these majestic creatures up close and personal. And, if you have children, introduce them to a few well-behaved adult Pyrs to gauge their reactions.

Space Requirements

Given enough exercise, the Pyr can adapt to small houses; however, it generally doesn't do well in apartments or condominiums. It is a breed that requires a certain amount of space and enjoys a yard. If you have a small home and you plan on doing some crate training with your dog—or providing a crate for the Pyr as its special place—be sure to carefully consider where you have a room in which to put an extra-large crate. Measuring 28 inches wide × 48 inches deep × 36 inches high (71 × 122 × 91 cm), this isn't a piece of equipment you can easily tuck unobtrusively in a corner of your living room, unless you're into cagelike end tables.

Extra-large dog beds also take up a substantial amount of floor space. The food and water bowls you will need are big, and the container you will need to store 40-plus pounds (18-plus kg) of dog food is even bigger.

What about transportation? You may be able to bring a puppy home in a medium-sized crate in the back seat of a tiny convertible, but a full-grown Pyr is a different story altogether. If you don't own a minivan, station wagon, or sport utility vehicle that can safely carry a super-sized crate, where are you going to put the dog? A Pyr may be able to lie down on a back seat of a sedan (which isn't very safe for the dog or the driver), but if you have two children buckled in the back, where will you put the dog?

Cleanup

While we're on the general subject of size, you may want to consider the cleanup requirements of a large dog. To put it bluntly, big dogs produce a lot of waste. You won't be able to carry a tiny plastic bag with you on your walks, and yard patrol will be a twice daily duty to keep things fresh and inoffensive to the neighbors.

Rental Problems

Most rental properties have weight restrictions for dogs—the most common being 20 pounds (9 kg)—a far cry from what your Pyr will weigh at maturity. And don't think you can sneak the dog in without someone noticing.

If you are renting a home that allows large dogs, you probably will be required to make a deposit (sometimes as much as one month's rent) and produce two letters from former neighbors saying what a responsible dog owner you are and how wonderful your dog is. (Of course, since you haven't purchased your Pyr yet, you can't say what a great dog it is—yet.) Some rental properties also charge a monthly surcharge of $20 to $50 per animal.

In addition, most property owners are extremely leery of new puppies. And even though large breeds, if given the proper attention and care, can be less destructive than small to medium-sized dogs, the rental owners don't understand this. They see "big dog" and translate that into "big problems."

Expenses

Because the Pyr is big, an owner can expect to pay more for the dog's basic care and maintenance than he or she would for an equally healthy dog of a smaller breed. Any medications or vaccinations that are based on a dog's body weight will be proportionally more for the Pyr; for example, expenses such as monthly heartworm preventive and flea and tick products can add up for a large dog.

The cost of food is substantially more for the Pyr than for a smaller dog, as are grooming bills, kennel boarding fees, and basic equipment, such as collars, crates, and other necessary dog items. It is estimated that a healthy,

problem-free, 40-pound (18-kg) dog costs about $500 a year. The Pyr is easily double to triple that amount. And that's just if it's healthy. (See Can You Afford a Pyr?, page 22.)

For those who live on a very tight budget, make sure you've allotted enough money for the care of your Pyr, and make sure you have an emergency fund set aside for unforeseen canine emergencies. If money is not a problem, you must still be sure that all family members agree that a Great Pyrenees is an appropriate expenditure—for the next 10 to 12 years.

Kids and Dogs

It's a myth that kids and dogs *just know* how to behave around each other. They don't. A

Well-trained Pyrs get along with well-behaved children, but, because of its size, your dog should not be left unattended with children under the age of five.

quick look at the most recent dog bite statistics from hospital emergency rooms will confirm that kids and dogs must be taught to respect each other.

If you are a parent—or a grandparent who has young children visiting often—you'll need to teach your growing puppy that even though a baby, toddler, or young child is at their eye level and may even be crawling on all fours, the child *is not a playmate* (in other words, no nipping, bumping, wrestling, biting, and so on).

In turn, your children must be taught to properly interpret a dog's body language and respect the dog's need for a place of its own. They must also know how to treat a dog with kindness and consideration.

Also, if your children are young (five and under), you must be able to provide 24-hour supervision of the dog and child. Problems can arise not only from dogs displaying dominance, possessiveness, or fear aggression, but also from the sheer size ratio of the dog to the child. It is very easy for a 100-pound (45-kg) dog to accidentally send a toddler for a good tumble. The rule: If you can't supervise closely, then separate. And if you can't separate, wait until your children are older and more responsible.

Is There a Pyr in Your Future?

You've read about the Pyr's good points and its challenging ones, you've met the breed in person and think they're lovely, and nothing about big dog ownership intimidates you. So, are you destined to be a Pyr owner?

Before you make that final decision to purchase a puppy or to adopt an adult Pyr, make an honest evaluation of yourself and your lifestyle and carefully assess whether owning a dog at this point in your life is a wise decision or one that should be postponed to a more opportune time. The following are some general lifestyle questions to consider.

What are your time restraints? Are you single and do you work long hours? Are you married and spend so much time shuttling your children to activities that you feel like an underpaid, overworked chauffeur? Or are you a single parent who's already stretched for time with your children? If you're feeling the squeeze for personal or family time, dog ownership may not be right for you *at this particular time.* Adult dogs take time; puppies require even more time. And to develop your Pyr puppy into the well-trained, loving family pet you want it to be takes *lots and lots of time.*

What kind of time? With a puppy, you'll have to clean out its crate every morning until it can "hold it" through the night. (You very well might have to clean the puppy every morning, too.) Then, there's the daily 20 minutes of obedience work, another 20 to 30 minutes for a walk, plus some playtime. Then there's the weekly brushing, monthly nail clipping, and perhaps a bath. Of course, if your puppy or adult tends to constantly run in the mud, your grooming may be daily and your floor mopping perpetual.

Raising a puppy is not easy. It involves the support and participation of the entire household—and it takes time.

Family Decisions. If you're single and live alone, then you don't need anyone's permission to buy a dog. However, if you're married, live with other adults, or have children, your situation immediately becomes more complex.

It is very important that before purchasing a dog, all family members agree not only on adding a dog to their home and lifestyle, but also which breed to add. If any family member expresses hesitation, don't gloss over it and hope for the best. It is far better to have an open discussion regarding the person's hesitation and clear the air. You may find that it is a simple problem that can be easily remedied to the satisfaction of everyone. On the other hand, the hesitation may be rooted in a more serious problem that cannot easily be rectified. Don't be put in a situation in which you have

Can You Afford a Pyr?

Dogs are expensive. Big dogs can be even more expensive. The following is a list of expenses you will incur in your first year of dog ownership.

Item	Cost
Folding crate; Giant-sized (28 inches W × 48 inches D × 36 inches H [71 × 122 × 91 cm])	$150
Pad for crate	50
Dog bed, 54 inches (137 cm), poly/cedar fill	75
Extra cover for bed	40
Baby gates (2)	80
Pet stain and odor remover (1 gallon [3.8 L])	20
Various chew toys	30
Anti-chewing spray (16-ounce spray)	7
Big-dog scoop	17
Dog food (quality)	400
Dog bowls (ceramic or no-tip stainless steel) (2)	20
Dental kit (toothbrush, toothpaste, finger brush)	6
Adjustable collars (2)	10
Matching 6-foot (1.8-m) leash	9
Personalized dog tag	5
Toenail clippers, styptic powder	17
Steel pin brush, comb, grooming scissors	12
Dog shampoo, conditioner (concentrated; 1 gallon [3.8 L])	35
Tick collars (2)	10
Flea and tick control (12 doses)	72
Heartworm preventive	120
Routine veterinary care	200
Obedience classes (10 months)	200
First Year Total	**$1,585**
Other: Fencing for yard (6-foot [1.8-m] privacy fence)	$300–$1,000+

Owning a big dog can run into big bucks.

to choose either a person or a dog unless you're ready to make that decision.

Also, if you are a parent, don't purchase a puppy or dog for a child with the idea that the child is entirely responsible for the dog. Ultimately, *you* are responsible for the dog. You can help your child be responsible and timely as far as dog-related chores, but if he or she fails miserably, the dog should never suffer.

Commitment Level. A steadfast commitment is the key component to making a dog relationship work. Answer this honestly: How committed are you to owning a dog? Are you willing to go the extra mile to meet your Pyr's needs and provide a safe, healthy, and happy environment? Or will you wither and give up as soon as your puppy presents a challenge to you?

If now is not the right time to own a dog, don't worry. It is far *better* to put off owning a Pyrenees until it is the *right* time and you have the energy, time, money, and just plain gumption to make dog ownership work.

If, however, this *is* a good time to own a dog, and your lifestyle is easily adaptable to adding a canine family member—and a Pyr would make the perfect pet—your next move is to choose a Pyrenees.

CHOOSING A GREAT PYRENEES

You're now at the point where you've weighed the pros and cons of owning a dog and have carefully considered the needs of a Great Pyrenees. Undaunted, you *still* want a Pyrenees. So, where do you begin to search for the Pyr of your dreams? The following are some points to consider on the who, what, where, when, and how of purchasing a puppy or dog that should help you to narrow your search.

Puppy versus Adult

When given the choice as to whether to buy a puppy or adopt or buy an adult, most dog owners naturally lean toward the more youthful choice: a puppy. And why not? Puppies are lots of fun and Great Pyrenees puppies are no exception. At eight or ten weeks, they resemble furry little polar bears. They're cute, they're cuddly, and they are *so* irresistible.

But, wait—puppies are irresistible for a reason: If they weren't so darn cute, most people would never be able to put up with them. Puppies are a lot of work. Puppy owners often find

Dam and pup in a moment of silent communication.

they have to remodel their homes with multiple baby gates so that the puppy can be kept in an area of least destruction. (Some owners also have to redecorate with new rugs and furniture after the puppy stage.) Puppy owners also must weather the teething storm, and diligently work on housebreaking. Then there are all the extra safety precautions that need to be made to spare breakables from a spurt of a puppy's high-energy romp around the house, not to mention the puppy-proofing that needs to be done to prevent the puppy from accidentally injuring or poisoning itself. And don't forget the constant training regime and a good dose of loving patience.

Benefits of Puppy Ownership

The benefits of puppy ownership, however, often outweigh the challenges. A pup can be a wise choice if the Pyr is a second pet or is coming into a home with children. (See The Pyr as a Second Pet, page 51.) A puppy is also a good choice if you are interested in competing in conformation with your Pyr or if you want a pup to train for livestock guardian work. The most important benefit, however, of purchasing a puppy is that *you* are in control of making sure the pup is raised appropriately, with solid training, good socialization skills, and proper habituation to everyday family and neighborhood lifestyles.

An Adult Dog

If owning a puppy sounds like a little too much work at this point in your life—and all you really want is a calm, wonderful, loving dog for a family pet—you might consider buying or adopting an adult Great Pyrenees. There are many wonderful Pyrs out there waiting for adoption, generally because their first owners either grew tired of dog ownership or didn't fully understand what owning a Great Pyrenees would be like and weren't ready to meet some of the challenges the breed can present. Adult dogs are often available from reputable breeders who responsibly take back their dogs that haven't worked out in their puppy homes. Another good source for adult dogs is through the GPCA's national breed rescue program (see Breed Rescue, page 38). A Great Pyrenees also may show up at your local shelter or pound.

Why an adult dog? Adult dogs have many redeeming qualities; in fact, some owners *prefer* to purchase or adopt an adult dog. Some adults make the transition easily; others need work. But, because the dog is an adult and its habits and challenges are known, you know what you're getting and what you're getting into . . . .

Note: Adult dogs require a good dose of patience. Expect your adopted Pyr to take at least a month before it adjusts to its new lifestyle.

If you are planning on adopting a Pyr, keep in mind that the quality of the placement, or making the match between dog and owner, relies on the quality of the placement organization. For example, GPCA rescue groups work very hard to make sure the right dog goes into the right home. Many nonprofit, private shelters work this way, too.

Other organizations, such as the local municipal pound, are often "first come, first served." In other words, if you're willing to adopt the dog and you can write a check, it is yours. In this situation, you would be well advised to proceed with extreme caution and enlist the help of a dog expert, such as a reputable Pyr breeder, a veterinarian, or a professional trainer. In this way, you can get a temperament and health assessment before adopting the dog.

Pet Quality or Show?

Back to puppies . . . If you want to purchase a Pyr as a pet only, then a pet-quality puppy is just what the doctor ordered. Pet quality means that the breeder does not feel that the puppy will make a good enough show dog to earn an AKC championship. This does not mean that the puppy isn't an outstanding-looking dog, or that the puppy won't have potential in performance events (agility, obedience, and others), or that it couldn't be trained to work as a livestock guardian dog. Quite the contrary. It just means that the puppy is not anticipated to have what it takes to win in the show ring. Period.

If you're interested in showing your Great Pyrenees, then you will *want* the best show-quality puppy you can afford; however, keep the following in mind as you write that check: A top-pick, show-quality puppy from one of the top breeders in the country or overseas is not a guarantee of owning the next Best in Show winner. Though your chances of having a real showstopper are greater buying a quality puppy from a recognized breeder, there is still an element of surprise in the whole deal. At the time of purchase, the pup's conformation appears to be very good and perhaps it has that extra-special "look" in the head that will catch the judge's eye. But, as all breeders know, the best-looking puppy at 8 to 10 weeks may not be the best-looking dog at 18 months. So do your homework and hope for the best.

A third type of puppy that you might find available in your area is one that comes from what is called "livestock guardian stock." Ranchers and farmers in some areas of the country have been very successful protecting their flocks from coyotes and wild dog packs with Pyrs trained for livestock guardian work. These dogs generally are not house dogs and are bred solely for livestock protection purposes. They have a tendency to be sharper, keener, and much more territorial than the average pet or show Pyr. If your intention is strictly to own a pet Pyrenees, Pyr breeders warn that a pup from livestock breeding may not make the easygoing, lovable pet you are looking for. If you are interested in a dual-purpose dog (show/guardian or pet/guardian), then this type of puppy may be of interest to you and may be worth looking into.

White or with Color?

If you're like most prospective pet Pyr owners, you'll say, "What? They're not all white?" Don't feel ignorant or uneducated. Most books available on the Great Pyrenees show all-white dogs or the photos are taken in black and white so you can't see the subtle markings of color. But yes, there are many Pyrenees out

there with patches of color ranging from reddish brown to a pale, creamy tan. If you are particularly fond of a certain coloration, this will limit your choices and may make your decision making a little simpler.

Male or Female?

Size: O.K., there's no such thing as a *small* Pyrenees, but females do run a little smaller than males in both height and weight. Females are typically about 85 pounds (38.5 kg) and are not generally taller than 29 inches (74 cm) at the shoulder. Males can run from 100 pounds (45 kg) and up, with an average height not exceeding 32 inches (81 cm). There are some bitches and dogs that will go over this standard, as well as those that will be smaller than the norm. So, if a relatively small Pyrenees is critical to you, be sure to tell the breeder.

Spay/neuter: If money is a factor, it generally costs less to neuter a male than to spay a female. If you own a pet-quality male or female, you should make plans to have it altered by the time it is six months old. Livestock guardian dogs should also be altered to prevent on-the-job distractions.

You won't want to spay or neuter, however, if you have purchased a show quality puppy with the intention of competing in the conformation ring. In this case, you will naturally want to delay any spaying or neutering until the dog has either shown it is or isn't a good show prospect.

Why spay or neuter? For one thing, if you own a pet quality puppy, you shouldn't be breeding it. By definition, the dog is lacking in some area and this fault should not be perpetuated. (Many breeders *require* a spay/neuter

Reputable breeders are honest and willing to share their advice freely. . .

contract to be signed by purchasers of *all* pet-quality dogs for this reason.) On the practical side, a female Pyr in season can be quite a mess, and a male Pyr can become a handful when it reaches adolescence between 10 and 20 months. Additionally, an altered dog is a healthy dog because it is not susceptible to many reproductive diseases or illnesses. The process will not automatically make your dog

. . . and they often raise their pups in a homelike setting.

fat and lazy; lack of exercise and too much food will do that!

Temperament: Males, particularly if they are intact, need a strong, clear hand from an owner who knows he or she is in charge. Once this leadership is established and a respect for the owner earned, males tend to be devoted, loving, and occasionally laid-back dogs.

Though females tend to look sweeter because of their smaller size and perhaps more refined heads, don't be fooled. Females can show as much dog-dog aggression as males, particularly when the other dog is a female Pyr.

Both males and females can be exceptionally tolerant of children when raised with them; but they are not playful dogs by nature. So if your children expect a lot of interaction with the dog and want it to retrieve balls and sticks and learn tricks, the Pyr will disappoint them.

Some livestock Pyrs may be a little too challenging for a first-time Pyr owner to purchase as a pet.

As a guardian, the Pyr will watch over your children and it will defend them with its life, but keep this protective nature in mind when your children's friends come to play. To the Pyr, other people's children are *not* considered family and the dog *may* try to keep them from entering your home.

Sources for Buying Pyrs

There are many places a person can buy a Pyr, some better than others. Buying a dog always involves some risk taking; however, with the right information, you can increase your chances of purchasing a Pyr that will fit well into your home and lifestyle.

Breeders

A breeder, by definition, is simply someone who breeds one dog to another. All breeders are not created equal—nor are their dogs. There are many subtle and not-so-subtle levels of breeding that can mean the difference between purchasing a Pyr with a beautiful temperament and sound conformation and buying an aggressive, dominating, unhealthy, and unsound Pyr.

Reputable, conscientious breeders: These are the breeders who agonize over every litter they breed. They are searching not only for the ideal Pyr in conformation, but also the ideal Pyr in every other way: health, soundness, working abilities, and temperament. These Pyr breeders take great pride in their dogs and are extremely careful when it comes to placing their puppies in homes. They are members of the national breed club and most likely members of a regional Pyr club. They are respected by other Pyr breeders, actively participate in conformation and performance events or train their Pyrs as working, livestock guardian dogs, and support breed rescue.

A breeder of this level will be able to provide you with a good puppy that meets your show, working, or pet needs. Most important to you is that a reputable breeder stands by what he or she breeds and will provide a health guarantee in writing, agreeing to replace a puppy or refund your money if the pup turns out to be unhealthy. The breeder will also take his or her dogs back at any age, for any reason. And, if you choose to go to a reputable breeder for your puppy, you will have an experienced person who will be happy to answer any questions you might have *for the life of the dog.*

Finding a reputable breeder can be a little tricky, since this breeder rarely advertises his or her litters in the newspaper. A good way to begin is by calling the GPCA breeder referral contact. This person will be able to provide you with names of reputable breeders in or near your area. Another good source for names is through the GPCA's national rescue chairperson. He or she will be able to tell you who stands behind their dogs and who doesn't, for the dogs of breeders who *aren't* reputable often end up in rescue (see Information, page 84, for addresses and phone numbers).

Buying from a reputable breeder, however, is not inexpensive. You can expect that a puppy from a very good breeder will cost as much as double the puppy from a less-reputable source. But don't think the reputable breeder is making any money from his or her more expensive pup. In most cases, the breeder actually loses money on every litter. Here's why.

The expenses of having a litter and caring for the bitch and puppies are quite high, if done right. The bill begins long before the pups are even born.

✔ First, there's prebirth expenses, which include prebreeding veterinary fees for the bitch, travel expenses and/or airline shipping to send the bitch to be bred to the stud dog, kenneling costs, and a stud fee.

✔ Then, there are the regular visits to the veterinarian during the bitch's pregnancy to make sure everything is well. When it is time, there are whelping costs. Most breeders construct a specialized whelping box and may have to take time off from work to supervise the whelping.

✔ If there are complications, it could mean an agonizing trip to the vet's office and more expenses.

✔ Once the puppies are born, there are all the routine, young puppy care expenses, which include quality puppy food, wormings, and two sets of vaccinations by the age of nine weeks.

✔ If there's anything that happens out of the ordinary—and there always is—that's an additional expense. It is not uncommon to have a stillborn puppy, problems with the delivery of a pup, or infections. Sometimes, even with the most experienced breeders and the most skilled veterinarians, puppies die and so do their mothers. (Imagine the exhaustion of trying to bottle-feed a newborn litter while your heart rests heavy with the loss of your favorite Pyr!)

If everything goes right, by the time the pups are ready to sell, the reputable breeder has literally hundreds of dollars invested in *each* puppy. You won't find this level of dedication with someone who is trying to make a quick profit or with someone who is inexperienced. But then again, breeders who don't make this kind of investment have compromised the health and welfare of their puppies—not to mention the satisfaction of any potential puppy owners.

Backyard breeders: This widely used term is a misnomer because many reputable breeders run their kennels in their backyards. The distinguishing difference between reputable breeders and "backyard" breeders is that the latter are inexperienced breeders with little, if any, real knowledge of the breed. Though these breeders are often well intentioned, they have relatively little experience with the breed and even less understanding as to how to breed for proper conformation, soundness, or temperament.

Generally, these breeders have puppies for one of several reasons:

1. It was an accident.

2. The owner wanted a puppy "just like Momma" and now has five others, too.

3. The owners wanted their children to experience the "miracle of life."

4. The owners thought they could make some money.

There are several drawbacks to buying a puppy from a source such as this. First of all, you will not receive a health guarantee, which is particularly important when these puppies have not been bred for good health. Second, you will not be able to return your dog at any time, for any reason. (This breeder does not have room for any extra dogs.) And third, the breeder will be of no help to you for any kind of breed advice. In fact, you'll probably know more about the breed than he or she does.

This is not to say that it is impossible to find a nice puppy from an inexperienced breeder. With a Pyrenees, however, a good temperament is paramount *and* responsible advice on how to train, handle, and raise a Great Pyrenees is crucial. If you purchase a Pyr from an inexperienced breeder, and that puppy turns out to have problems—either physical or mental—be prepared to deal with it on your own. Buying from a backyard breeder is certainly a "buyer-beware" sort of situation.

Pet Stores

It used to be a common sight at pet stores across the country to walk in and find a kennel full of puppies for sale. This sight is becoming rarer and rarer, since most pet stores do not have the resources to offer health guarantees or lifetime "return" policies. There are some pet stores that do still offer puppies for sale, however, and the quality of these puppies can vary greatly.

If you choose to buy a puppy through a pet store, be sure to ask for the name and phone

number of the puppy's breeder. If the store won't give you the breeder's name, then ask for a copy of the puppy's pedigree. Take the pedigree to a knowledgeable Pyr breeder, your local all-breed dog club, or even your veterinarian, and see if anyone is familiar with the puppy's parents, the bloodlines, or the breeder.

If you get the breeder's name, call him or her about the puppy you are interested in as well as the puppy's parents. If the breeder is in your area, ask if you can come out and meet the mother. (The father may or may not be on the premises.) Temperament is largely hereditary, so it's a good idea to check everything you can. Also, be sure to ask the breeder for a veterinary

To a puppy, the world is a playground and all objects, even a garden hose, are its toys.

referral—and then call the veterinarian. If the breeder can't provide you with a veterinarian's name, he or she has most likely been skimping on veterinary care—not a good sign.

If everything checks out, great! You may have found a nice, pet-quality Pyr. However, if the pet store will not reveal the breeder's name or if the pedigree is unrecognizable, the pet store has probably bought the puppy from a disreputable breeder or, worse yet, a puppy mill

(see below). If this is the case, you will know that you are dealing with a dog that was not bred well and may be susceptible to all sorts of mental and physical problems. Again, a buyer-beware situation.

Unscrupulous Breeders

For this breeder, profit reigns. Though the puppy mills that splashed the pages of popular magazines and were the subject of exposés in years past have not received as much adverse publicity lately, they are still out there. There are still people who breed and sell dogs in much the same way as poorly kept livestock. Often, little or no money is spent on preventive

To determine what sort of temperament a puppy has, watch as it plays with littermates.

and/or maintenance veterinary care. No dogs are tested for hip or eye problems, and breeding records are shaky or nonexistant. The object of this individual is to breed as many sellable puppies as feasible and to move them as quickly as possible with no concern for health, soundness, or temperament. Some dog farmers use the services of puppy brokers to "move" their litters.

Regardless of what method these people use to sell their puppies, they should be avoided as a source for a healthy Pyr. In fact, if the conditions are bad enough, the breeder and the suspected situation should be reported to your local Animal Control office and a contact made with the nearest Great Pyrenees Club of America rescue. There are legal actions that can be taken against cruel and inhumane treatment of animals and perhaps the operation can be shut down.

Visiting the Breeder

The time has come and you find yourself sitting in front of a litter of adorable Great Pyrenees puppies. Your goal, of course, is to pick a beautiful puppy that is healthy and has a wonderful temperament, but how do you even begin to decide?

First of all, the entire litter may be there for you to see, but typically many puppies—if not most—are already spoken for. Often potential owners make deposits on puppies that haven't even been born yet, particularly if the breeding is expected to be exceptionally good. Second, you should already have a few criteria in mind that will help you narrow down the crowd, such as the type of pup you want (pet, show, or working), the sex, and a color preference, if any. Beyond that, the decision making can be tough—but not impossible.

A few pointers that should help you in choosing the perfect Pyr are:

General Inspection

When you first walk in to see the litter of puppies, take a look at the general health of the mother and the puppies. Is their area clean and dry? Do the mother and litter appear to be happy and healthy? Check to make sure the kennel or yard is clear of any signs of vomiting and diarrhea, both of which could indicate health problems.

Before you start playing with the puppies, make sure you take time to meet the mother. (Many females can be protective of their puppies, so you will want to see the mother when she is away from her pups.) If the father is on site, ask to meet him, too. However, don't be concerned too much if the father is not on the premises; females are often shipped to be bred to the males. Is the mother of the pups a good example of the breed standard? Is she friendly? Timid? Aggressive? Unsocialized? The mother's temperament can be an indicator of what you might encounter with some of her pups.

Puppy Inspection

Temperament: Watch the entire litter as they play together. How do the puppies act around one another? Does one puppy tend to boss the others around? A puppy that is very pushy with its littermates may have the potential for developing dominance or aggression problems. If you are working with a reputable breeder, he or she will be able to tell you if this might be a problem or if what you are seeing is just a very playful puppy.

Once you've watched the pups' behavior with one another, ask the breeder to separate the puppies you are interested in from the ones you've ruled out. This will help you make your decision. If you've decided you want a snow white female, for example, this could eliminate more than half the puppies in the litter; it's much easier to pick a puppy from two or three choices than ten or more.

Sit down with the pups you're interested in and play with them. How do they react to you?

Do any puppies hang back timidly or seem otherwise frightened of you? If so, they may be shy and probably aren't a good choice. On the other hand, are there any puppies that just won't leave you alone and insist that you pet them? Be wary of the first puppy that jumps in your lap; this pup may be too confident and may try to exert its rank later on in life. The "middle" puppies (not shy, but not the boldest either) are usually the best choices for a good pet Pyr. Look for a happy, playful puppy, which the majority of the litter should be.

Physical: When you are handling the puppies, check them for general health.

✔ The puppies' eyes, ears, noses, and other body orifices should be clear of discharges and inflammation.

✔ The puppies' coats should be thick, soft, and healthy, not dry. A bloated, thin-coated, sluggish puppy might be infested with worms or otherwise ill.

✔ The skin beneath the coat should be smooth and healthy and shouldn't have any signs of scabbing, bleeding, or crustiness. While you're studying the puppies' coat, be sure to look for any puncture wounds or signs of injections.

✔ Check for fleas and ticks.

✔ As you feel each puppy, make sure the puppies don't have any lumps or bumps.

✔ Look to see if the puppies' legs and spine appear to be straight and that the upper and lower jaws match.

✔ Overall, does the puppy look symmetrical? Are its ears and eyes set properly?

Health Records

Puppies generally need to be wormed within the first four weeks after birth. Also, by eight weeks, the puppies should have received their first vaccinations for distemper, hepatitis, parvovirus and coronavirus. If the puppies are older, they also should have received their second set of shots.

If the puppies have not received the appropriate vaccinations and wormings, they are at serious health risk until a veterinarian can assess their health. If you purchase a puppy that has *not* received the appropriate veterinary care, make sure you have a written statement from the breeder that you can bring the puppy back if it has (or develops) any serious health problems. If you cannot get this guarantee in writing, beware!

Legalese

The sort of paperwork you will be asked to sign varies from breeder to breeder. Optimally, if a breeder stands behind his or her puppies, you should receive a contract that guarantees the good health of your puppy. The breeder should agree to exchange your puppy for another, or give you your money back if the puppy should develop a serious illness or problem within a specified time.

The breeder should also give you the puppy's papers (AKC registration form) *when you buy the pup*. The breeder registers the litter with the AKC. You must register the puppy as its owner. If the breeder says he or she will send the registration form in the mail, don't get your hopes up of ever seeing them; you probably won't. Keep in mind, too, that an AKC registration is not a symbol of quality nor a guarantee of health. It is simply proof that a particular litter is of a particular breed and documents its pure (same breed) heritage.

Pedigree: When you purchase your puppy, you should also receive a breeder's copy of the

pup's pedigree, which should show three generations of the pup's family tree, along with registration numbers and any titles, such as conformation championships and performance titles, that are recognized by the AKC, and certain health certifications the pup's parents and other relatives have received.

A breeder's pedigree can be more detailed, going back several more generations and packed with extra information, such as both domestic and foreign titles won by the pup's

Males and females are similar in temperament, but vary in size, with males weighing in up to 20 pounds more than their sizable female counterparts.

ancestors, and other details such as the coloration and markings of every dog on the pedigree.

Most breeders are exceptionally proud of their puppies and will be happy to share all sorts of interesting information about your

Adult dogs can be excellent companions if given a good chance to adjust to their new homes.

puppy's heritage. Note also that if you are dealing with a less-than-reputable breeder, what the pedigree says and what is actually the truth may be quite different.

Spay/neuter contract: If the puppy you are buying is considered pet quality, you may be required to sign a spay/neuter contract and the breeder may hold the pup's registration papers until your veterinarian sends the breeder a signed certificate that your dog was altered.

Limited registration: You may also be given papers for a Limited Registration of your new puppy. This registration prevents you from showing your dog in conformation or breeding your dog, but you will be able to enter your dog in most AKC performance events. The idea behind this registry is to encourage responsible dog ownership and the spaying or neutering of your dog.

Co-ownership: If you have chosen a very, very good Pyr, you may be asked to share the puppy; the breeder may ask if you'd like to be a co-owner. Co-ownership helps the breeder retain some control over the future of a particular Pyr. It is important, if you want a happy co-ownership, that you get along well with the breeder and share the same visions for the puppy. Both you and the breeder should sign a contract spelling out the conditions of the agreement.

The First Stop

It is always a good idea to schedule a veterinary exam as soon as possible for your new puppy. As a trained professional, your veterinarian will be able to give your puppy a comprehensive health exam and get you started on a proper vaccination and preventive medicine schedule. Throughout the dog's life, your vet-erinarian will be an invaluable source of information on general dog health and behavior.

Adopting an Adult Pyrenees

Breed Rescue

If you are looking for an adult Great Pyrenees, Pyr Rescue is a great way to find a loving pet. Pyr Rescue is run by experienced Pyr breeders and owners who have extensive breed experience. The dogs are given complete veterinary exams, are backed by a health guarantee (you can return or exchange the dog if it has serious health problems), have been evaluated for temperament, and are ready for a loving home.

Contrary to what many people believe, most Pyrs turned into Rescue are neither troublemakers nor are they unhealthy. (Rescue carefully evaluates all relinquished Pyrs and euthanizes any that are dangerous or critically ill.) The adult Pyrs you will find here are often from very nice homes that just didn't quite work out, and are eager to devote themselves to a *new*, lifelong owner.

If you are interested in adopting a rescued Pyr, be prepared to be carefully screened by the rescue organization. You will be required to answer a questionnaire and may be subject to a home visit by Rescue volunteers. Do not be offended. The Rescue workers want to make sure that their Pyrs find good, *permanent* homes. After you have been approved for a Pyr, you may have to wait a few weeks until a good match is available. Be patient and keep in mind that the Rescue group knows what it is doing; you will get your Pyr. And you will also get that terrific feeling that goes along with saving a life.

Pet Adoption Fairs

A growing trend among pet stores is to offer pet fairs to which breed clubs and rescue organizations can bring their dogs for prospective owners to meet. This is a good way to meet responsible breeders and learn about a particular breed. It is also an excellent place to meet the Great Pyrenees Breed Rescue chairman for your area and candidly discuss the pros and cons of adopting an adult dog.

Shelters and Pounds

Pyrs—both puppies and adults—can show up in the local shelter or pound, but if you choose to adopt a dog from this source, be careful. Make sure you talk at great length with the shelter workers or volunteers who have been caring for the dog about the dog's general health and temperament. Read through the questionnaire that the surrendering owner filled out when he or she dumped the Pyr at the shelter. Keep in mind that owners often "fudge" or outright lie on their answers. Sometimes owners will say things to help the dog find a home, such as saying it's housebroken when it's not. Other times, the owners will do the reverse—to justify giving up a perfectly good pet, the previous owner may write that the dog is aggressive when it is really very sweet.

Ideally, you should take a dog expert, such as a trainer, an experienced Pyr breeder, or a Pyr Rescue person with you to help you in your assessment of the dog's temperament, trainability, and general health. Be sure to schedule time to take the dog away from the shelter on a walk or in a fenced play area so you and your dog expert can better judge what its temperament is like.

If you have children, a shelter Pyr may not be the best choice. A known commodity from a source such as a reputable breeder or Pyr Rescue that has had the dog long enough to know its temperament is probably a better choice. If you do adopt a Pyr from a shelter, expect the worst until the dog proves itself. Begin your obedience training immediately and *never, ever* leave the dog alone with small children. Remember, one bite can scar a lifetime. You just can't be too cautious.

Think It Over

Whether purchasing a puppy or an adult, you should be very comfortable and pleased with your decision. If for any reason you are uneasy with the breeder, or if you have any sort of misgivings about the pup or adult you have selected, wait. It's not a bad idea to think things over. Remember that your new puppy or dog will be a partner for life, so hold out for that perfect Pyr.

BRINGING YOUR PYR HOME

The day is quickly arriving for you to pick up your new Pyr puppy. Or you are on the waiting list for a rescued adult, which could arrive any day! Are you ready?

The First Day

Whether you've chosen a puppy or an adult, your first few days are bound to be hectic. In planning for this, make sure you have arranged to pick up your puppy on a Friday or Saturday, so that if you work away from home you can at least have a few days off to help your new family member adjust. Even better, you might consider arranging a few days off from work. This way, even though you'll undoubtedly be prepared for *most* of what your new Pyrenees will throw at you, a few extra days off will help you make sure your Pyr settles in with the least amount of hassles and disturbances.

Of course, before bringing your new Pyr home, you'll want to be prepared. You'll save yourself a lot of potential headaches *and* you'll be able to make your home a successful environment for your new puppy or adult. Preparation includes stocking up on all the right supplies, and preparing your home, yard, and family for the canine arrival.

Your puppy will be eager to explore its new surroundings.

Supplies to Get in Advance

One of the most common things a new dog owner does is forget to purchase the essential supplies for the new puppy or dog's first night at home. For example, many puppy buyers show up at the breeder's house with no collar, leash, or travel crate for the new puppy. Or, in their surprise and excitement, new puppy owners often forget to purchase food, or have no secure place, such as a properly sized crate, for the puppy to sleep in. Make sure you have the important supplies you'll need well in advance of your new dog's arrival.

The Veterinary Check

In addition, you'll want to schedule some very important appointments and classes. If possible, you should schedule a veterinary appointment for the day you pick up your puppy or adult. At most, don't allow more than 48 hours to go by without having a veterinary check. The sooner you can have your veterinarian give your pup a clean bill of health, the better!

If you do find that your pet has some health concerns, having this diagnosis made immediately can help you to take appropriate action. Serious health situations may justify returning the puppy to the breeder. (If you have a written health guarantee, this should be no problem.) If there is a problem, early diagnosis of conditions and diseases might increase the pet's chances of recovery.

Enrolling in a Training Program

Another action you'll want to take those very first days (or even the weeks before the dog's arrival) is to enroll in a good training program (see Finding a Good Training School, page 73). Classes for puppies begin as soon as the pup has received its second round of vaccinations, at eight to ten weeks. Adults may begin novice classes at any age.

Whether you're purchasing a puppy or adopting an adult, much of your human-canine success will depend on your commitment to training your dog. The investment of a year of training classes for a puppy or an adult dog is well worth the small fee you will have to pay.

Identification: Tags, Chips, and Tattoos

No one plans on losing a puppy or a new dog on the first day that it is brought home. But this happens all the time, and to the best-intentioned dog owners, too. So be prepared. You've got the collar, the leash, now you need some identification.

Tags: Even if you don't have a name picked out, this is no excuse not to have a tag ready.

Simply engrave the tag with the breed name and your phone number. It may sound silly to put "I am a Great Pyrenees" on the tag; however, many people do not know what a Great Pyrenees is, particularly a puppy. A misidentification can lead to confusion when trying to locate or even claim your Pyrenees.

Microchips: Although you can't purchase this means of identification before the pup's arrival home, you may want to consider having a microchip implanted in your dog as a more permanent means of identification.

A microchip is a tiny device that is inserted with a syringe below the surface of the dog's skin. Each chip has its own identification number, which can be read when a scanner is passed over it. To identify a lost dog, a veterinarian or shelter worker scans the dog for a microchip and the number will appear in the scanner (assuming scanner and microchip are compatible). The "finder" then calls an 800 number, provides the chip registry with his or her identification number, and gives the registry the number of the microchip. The microchip service, which holds owner contact information in a data base, then tells the veterinarian or other identified caller how to contact the lost dog's owner. If all works well, the dog is returned to the owner. A drawback of the microchip is that the systems are not universal. In other words, not all scanners can read all chips.

Tattoos: A tattoo is a permanent form of identification that can be performed by your veterinarian or other person trained

A puppy gate will keep your new arrival out of mischief.

in the technique. A series of numbers tattooed on your dog is registered with a national registry that retains information on the dog and its owner. If someone finds the dog and discovers the tattooed numbers, the chances are good that your dog will be returned to you if the finder contacts a shelter or a veterinarian.

A drawback to tattoos is that the tattoo—usually on the inside thigh or ear flap—cannot be seen easily.

Preparing for the New Dog

No one can ever be totally prepared for the arrival of a new puppy, and even the arrival of an adult dog into a new home has its challenges. However, certain preparations and precautions can help make your Pyr's transition go as smoothly as possible. You will have to Pyr-proof your house, yard, and family.

Preparing Your Home

If you've recently had babies or toddlers in your home, you know that *nothing* within crawling or standing reach is safe. Everything that is within reach of a young human is

Nontip bowls: Back, plastic; front, metal with rubber rim.

Supply Checklist

Essentials/First Day

1. **Crate:** Your Pyr will need a crate for car travel and as a cozy, secure sleeping spot. Line the bottom of the crate with a blanket or towel with the mother's or the breeder's scent.

2. **Cuddle Doll and Toy:** Make sure they are washable and don't contain any parts that might be choking hazards.

3. **Collar and Leash:** Flat buckle or quick snap kinds are best, made of leather, cotton, or nylon web. Adjustable collars will allow you to keep a collar longer while your puppy is growing through the sizes. No choke chains or collars! A sturdy 6-foot (1.8-m) leash. Retractable leashes are good *after* the puppy is leash-trained (and won't drag you off).

4. **Food and Water Bowls:** Heavyweight, nontipping bowls are best.

5. **Food:** Good-quality puppy food, preferably what the breeder has been feeding, to avoid new-food tummy upsets.

6. **Identification:** A dog tag with your phone number is fine for the first day. Later, you may want to look into more permanent means of identification, such as microchipping or tattooing (see Identification: Tags, Chips, and Tattoos, page 42).

7. **Dog Bed:** Preferably, one that has a removable, washable cover.

8. **Pooper-scooper:** Big jobs require the correct equipment.

9. **Grooming Supplies:** Wire brush, dematting comb, trimming scissors, toenail clippers, and dog shampoo.

It's amazing how quickly a young puppy can get into trouble the instant you let it out of your sight.

Be sure to ask your veterinarian what poisonous plants are indigenous to your area, and if you find any in your yard, remove them promptly.

touched, pulled, and put in the mouth for a taste test. With puppies and new dogs, the curiosity factor is much the same as it is for little humans, except that dogs have teeth.

In order to safeguard your house and your new Pyr as well as possible, do what new parents do: Get down on your hands and knees and check your home for ordinary household items that could be dangerous in the mouth or paws of a puppy or curious adult.

Electrical cords: Chomping through a live electrical cord will do more than give your bobtail its first home perm. The jolt it could receive from this feat could be deadly. Also, a partial chewing of the cord could create a fire hazard. Beyond the electrical charge, a cord is typically attached to something of value, such as a lamp, which you may not want your Pyrenees to smash into a million pieces by pulling

on the cord. To avoid electrical cord accidents, keep all cords out of reach or securely covered.

Knickknacks: A Pyr can easily knock the fragile figurines off a coffee table or send an untethered curio cabinet careening to the floor. To protect your investments and sentimental curios, either keep the dog away from areas with breakables or put the items in a more secure place.

Toys: My toys, your toys, its toys—who can tell the difference? A Pyr can't. Kids need to pick up their toys or the door to the playroom should be shut. Puppies and adults alike enjoy a good chew, particularly if it smells like someone they love. If toys are accessible, your children will soon find headless action figures and remodeled dollhouses. Also, jagged, half-chewed plastic pieces, as well as dangerously sharp items, can be choking hazards for the dog to swallow.

Your stuff: Again, if it smells like you and it's just lying around, your puppy or dog will most likely want to play with it. This includes shoes (they don't have to be leather), socks, underwear, bathrobes, even books, files, and computer disks. Keep them out of reach.

Food: If you're not used to an animal that can make a clean swipe of a dinner for four that you *just* put on the table—and still act like it's hungry for dinner—then you're in for a shock. A full-grown Great Pyrenees will be able to reach anything that is at table or counter height. The only food that can be safely left out in the open is food that is put on top of the refrigerator. Just don't leave a chair too close by.

Besides the annoyance of having your dinner stolen, allowing your Pyr to eat your food can be dangerous for your dog, too. *Salmonella* bacteria can be found in raw chicken and can make your dog very ill. Foods that are high in salts can cause vomiting; dried foods that can expand in a dog's stomach can cause severe bloating. Other foods, such as baking chocolate, can be lethal.

In general, keep your dog's food and yours safely contained and out of reach.

Garbage: The easiest way to keep your puppy or dog out of the garbage is to keep the garbage locked up—literally. If your pup figures out how to open the under-the-sink cabinet doors, bungee-cord them shut.

Medicines, cleaning fluids, and poisons: Your Great Pyrenees can't read labels, but it most likely will be able to outsmart any child-proof packaging manufacturers can produce. To keep your Pyr safe, store all medications, household cleaning solutions, poisons, fertilizers, weed killers, and other hazardous items out

A good fence is a must for all Pyrs.

of reach and/or behind securely shut doors. Search your home and garage for any insect or rodent poisons and remove them. Both contain poisons that can kill your dog.

Also, be sure to clean up any antifreeze that may have spilled on the garage floor or driveway. Antifreeze tastes sweet to animals and is therefore attractive to dogs, but it only takes a small amount to kill your Pyr.

Poisonous plants: If you come home and you find your puppy has eaten an entire houseplant, what should you do? Do you know if this plant is poisonous or not? Do you even know what kind of plant it was? If not, you need to rescue a leaf or two (if possible) and take your pet to the veterinarian immediately.

Toxic reactions to poisonous plants can range from rashes in the mouth to extreme swelling of the mouth and throat that cause the dog to asphyxiate. Other plants can cause vomiting, abdominal pain, and tremors, as well as heart, respiratory, and kidney problems.

Checklist

Poisonous Plants
Below is a brief listing of some of the more commonly encountered poisonous plants that are grown inside the house or in the yard. For a complete listing of poisonous indoor and outdoor plants and their level of toxicity, consult your veterinarian.

✔ Amaryllis
✔ Asparagus Fern
✔ Azalea
✔ Bird of Paradise
✔ Boston Ivy
✔ Caladium
✔ Chrysanthemum
✔ Daffodil
✔ Delphinium
✔ Elephant Ear
✔ Poinsettia
✔ Yew

To avoid accidentally poisoning your puppy or dog, remove any poisonous plants from your home *and your garden.* Also, give a wary eye to any floral arrangements you might receive. Many of the flowers used in these arrangements can be harmful, too.

Preparing Your Yard
Though your yard may seem to be a safe haven for your new puppy or adult, be sure to give it a good once-over before your puppy or dog arrives.

Fencing: This is a necessity if you are to keep a Great Pyrenees safely. If you don't have a fenced backyard, fence it in. A sturdy wood privacy fence is attractive; however, a tall, chain-link fence can work as well. As previously mentioned, invisible fencing does not work well with a Pyr that will bear the pain to burst through the electric barrier. The fence also allows stray dogs and other animals to enter the Pyr's territory.

If you already have a fence, make sure to take a walk around the perimeter, checking for broken or loose boards, exposed nails, or holes. Keep your fence safe and secure for your new pet.

Landscaping: How much do you value your current landscaping? If you've poured a small fortune into it, you may want to keep your Pyr away from it—permanently. Pyrs *love* to dig, especially during hot, summer months.

Remove all toxic plants from your yard before you bring your puppy home.

Preparing Family Members

Lay down the laws before the dog arrives. Will the puppy or adult be allowed on the furniture, or must it stay on the floor? Will the dog be restricted to the kitchen, or can it be given greater access to the house? To prevent future complications or arguments, make sure all family members (including regular sitters or nannies) know what the dog can or can't do, where it can or can't be, and who is responsible for what dog chores, and which adult will be spearheading the dog's training efforts.

Welcome Home

The first day home with a puppy or a rescued adult is one of sheer joy; your long-awaited treasure is finally home. The bonding process begins and you are on your way to a loving relationship. But life isn't all roses with a growing puppy or with an adult dog trying to adjust to its new surroundings; it has its ups and downs.

The First Day

When you get home, the first introductions you should make to your Pyr are: Where to go potty (outside), where to get a drink (water bowl), where dinner is served (food bowl), and where to take naps (the crate).

Then you can introduce your puppy or adult to the rest of its home life. Depending on where your Great Pyrenees came from, it may or may not be familiar with mirrors, glass windows, or screens. A toilet flushing may be an unusual sound, too. Most curious puppies and dogs will take all these new experiences in stride, but a Pyr that is a little on the fearful side will need to be supported with lots of pos-

TIP

Rules for Children

If you have children, you will also want to brief them as to the rules of behavior around a puppy or dog. If you don't feel you are getting through to your children, you might ask your veterinarian or the breeder to talk to your kids. Many times, advice that comes from a respected third party sinks in a lot faster.
✔ No roughhousing or teasing allowed.
✔ Leave the dog alone while it is sleeping. Awaken it by calling its name.
✔ A Pyrenees is large, but cannot be ridden like a pony.

itive encouragement to prevent any bad first experiences.

If you've brought home a puppy, you may be tempted to play all day, but you must remember to allow your puppy to take its much-needed naps. If you've invited friends, neighbors, or family members to come over and meet the puppy, it is especially important to remember the pup's need for rest. It's a good idea to keep the crate door open while your puppy is up and playing so that any time it wants to escape for a nap or just a little peace it can run into the crate and curl up.

Adult dogs need their rest, too, so even though yours may be a bundle of energy, be sure to provide it with a nice, quiet place should it want a retreat. Don't overwhelm your new dog. Adults often take a little more adjusting to new surroundings than their younger counterparts, so be patient.

The First Night

When night falls and it's time for you to hit the hay, don't be surprised if your Pyr doesn't. Both adults and puppies will have some adjusting to do, but part of your dog's success in settling into home life will be how well you can stick to your schedule.

Before you put your puppy or dog in its crate for the night, be sure to let your Pyrenees relieve itself and get one last drink if it wants to. Put one or two toys in the crate and a nice blanket to snuggle up in—and one that can be washed in the morning. Then put your Pyr in its crate. As you head for bed, your puppy (or adult) will undoubtedly tell you just how unfair and unjust you are for leaving it behind. That's O.K. Keep walking.

Multiple Pyrs can and do get along, but pet owners are advised to match males with females for the best chance of success.

Separation Anxiety

As you lie awake in bed, listening to the irritating sounds of a puppy crying, or the bigger sounds of an adult howling or barking, remember: This is natural. A puppy will cry because it is away from its mother and littermates. An adult will vocalize because it is unfamiliar with its new surroundings. Some puppies and adults will be more vocal than others. Regardless, be prepared for a sleepless night. In fact, prepare yourself for a sleepless week. It will take time for your Pyr to adjust to its new surroundings. The good news is that this stage doesn't last forever.

If you've bought a puppy, do keep your puppy in its crate at night and don't bring it into bed with you to comfort it. Soiled bedsheets are no fun, nor is the future thought of a fully grown Great Pyrenees hogging the bed every night. It is O.K., however, to keep the pup's crate in your room, if that is where you plan on letting your pet sleep eventually. And it is fine during the night to check on your puppy, let it out to relieve itself, reassure it that you love it, and put it back into its crate.

If you've brought home an adult and plan to allow it to sleep in your bedroom with you, it is still advisable to use the crate method for the first several nights or weeks. You'll know exactly where your dog is and there won't be any accidents or destructiveness.

The Morning After

You may feel as if you haven't slept a wink. But guess what? That cute little puppy is fully rested and raring to go. (This also goes for an adult that has been crated all night.) If you let it out several times during the night, you may have a clean crate and a clean puppy. Most likely, however, your pup will have a soiled crate and paws to match with which to greet you. Open the crate, scoop your puppy up, and whisk it outside to relieve itself, then take a deep breath, remember to be patient, clean out the pup's crate, clean up your puppy, and remind yourself once again that this is a temporary stage. Once the pup settles into its new routine, it will cry or bark only during the night when it wants to get out of its crate to relieve itself outside. When the pup is older, it may begin its nightly guardian duties and bark excessively, but that's another issue (see Discouraging Barking, page 78).

Important Puppy Phases

Though these phases are typically approached while the Pyr is a puppy, if you adopt an adult dog, you will undoubtedly have to work with your dog on one or more qualities to make it a good canine partner.

Socialization

With people: In order for your puppy to grow up to be a well-behaved and sociable canine, it must learn that all people, regardless of their size, sex, age, or race, are to be liked. The only way to teach your pup this is to

Arrange your schedule so you can maximize your time with your Pyr. It will be a puppy only once!

introduce it to as many different people as possible. Since behaviorists believe that the critical period for socializing a puppy begins roughly around four weeks of age and continues through the first month with its new owner (12 weeks old), it is crucial that you begin your pup's socialization immediately.

✔ Take your puppy on walks in public places.

✔ Put your puppy on a *sit-stay* (see Sit, p. 74) and give the mail carrier and meter reader a biscuit to give to your puppy.

✔ Teach your puppy to *stand-stay* (see Stand-Stay, page 75) and have friends examine your pup's ears, teeth, and paws.

All these exercises will help your puppy to grow up to become a well-adjusted, social adult.

With other dogs: It is equally important for your Pyr to understand how to behave properly around other dogs. To do this, your puppy should be frequently introduced to other dogs in a controlled setting. One of the best ways to begin working on canine socialization is by enrolling in a puppy kindergarten (see Why Train Early?, page 73). The instructors will be able to assist you in training your dog to obey you when other dogs are nearby.

Habituation

Another important learning phase for your puppy involves familiarizing it with daily life in and away from your home. If you take your pup with you wherever you go, you should have little trouble accustoming your puppy to the sounds of traffic, garbage trucks, travel in the car, the daily route of the mail carrier, children on bicycles (they are not to be chased), and such natural occurrences as thunderstorms, wind, and heavy rain. The puppy may initially be startled by these stimuli; however, after it has been exposed to these occurrences time after time with no bad consequences and rewards for calm, good behavior, the puppy will gradually learn to accept them.

It is important to remember during any habituation work that a dog should never be punished for displaying a fearful reaction to a stimulus, such as a passing car. Also, a fearful response should not be rewarded with food or praise or comforting. Basically, it should be ignored. When the dog reacts calmly to the stimulus, then and only then should it be rewarded with praise or treats.

Teething

Between three and five months, your puppy will begin to lose its puppy teeth and break in its permanent teeth. During this phase, your puppy is teething and has a need to chew. The erupting adult teeth can cause discomfort, itching, and swelling. Most puppies, unlike teething children, don't show much irritability; however, they do have an almost uncontrollable desire to chew—and, they'll chew on anything.

Have patience. This phase will pass and the desperate urge to chew will subside. However, while you're waiting for it to pass, make sure you have lots of sturdy teething toys for your puppy and that you keep it from getting into trouble. In other words, this is not the time to accidentally forget to crate your puppy; you could come home to gnawed baseboards and kitchen cabinets or a three-legged dining room table. Also, if you have young children who don't like to be used as teething toys, you may want to separate them from the puppy during its chewing phase, or at least supervise their play extremely closely.

A Successful Relationship

The keys to having a successful dog-owner relationship are founded in the initial relationship you develop with your Pyr. If you have a puppy, you must be prepared for anything. You must also be firm, and above all, be loving. Remember, your Pyr will be a puppy only once.

If you have selected an adult, you will be confronted with fewer, but perhaps different, challenges while you help your new friend make the transition to your home and activities.

Remember, with both puppies and adults, the time you spend with your Pyr nurturing and training it will be repaid to you a hundredfold. It is an investment well worth making.

The Pyr as a Second Pet

As an only pet, the Pyr can be unparalleled in gentleness and loyalty toward its immediate family. It can also be exceptionally tolerant when raised with small children. Small pets, such as rabbits, birds, and even cats, often are not a problem when introduced to the Pyr as a puppy. It is thought that the Pyrenees views these smaller, helpless animals as part of the flock it needs to protect; however, you should still supervise your puppy's interaction with other pets at least until the pup is approximately 18 months old.

Where is there a problem? With other dogs, particularly same-sex Pyrs. Pairing a male Pyr with another male Pyr is virtually impossible, say breeders, and the fights can be ferocious. Female Pyrs paired with other females may have a little better chance of success, but this often can be as disastrous as the male-male pairing. Troubles usually don't begin until the youngest Pyr hits adolescence or even adulthood.

Interestingly, however, Pyrs can often be paired with smaller breeds quite successfully, and with medium-size breeds if the other dog does not have a dominant temperament. This acceptance of non-alpha or smaller dogs probably goes back to the days when Pyrs worked for shepherds as a team with small herding dogs. The small teammate was tolerated (and even protected) but all other animals were considered predators.

So, if you are adding a Pyr as a second dog, make sure you discuss your situation in detail with your breeder and knowledgeable Pyr owners. Listen objectively to what they have to say. If you add a Pyr to your family, it shouldn't be at the expense of any pets you already own.

If you already own a Pyr and want another, be very careful. Opposite-sex matches (be sure to spay and neuter) are most likely to succeed and the dogs can make great companions for each other. Again, talk to those who have extensive experience handling multiple Pyrs and then decide if two Pyrs are really better than one.

BASIC CARE AND NUTRITION

A well-groomed, well-fed, conditioned Great Pyrenees is a sight to behold. The dog's coat is glossy, its eyes clear and sharp, and its demeanor exudes good health. Both young and older Pyrs can look this good if you make the effort to give them the very best in care. If you maintain your Pyr in good health, you'll help it live a full, disease-free life.

Grooming

Grooming involves caring not only for your Pyr's lustrous coat, but also its eyes, ears, teeth, and nails. Some Pyrs will require more grooming attention than others. For example, a Pyr that is outside much of the day may get into more trouble with dirt and mud than a Pyr that is mostly indoors. Some dogs are born with teeth that require little extra care; others need a good brushing every few days to prevent plaque from building up. Some Pyrs grow nails more quickly than others and require regular clipping; other dogs' nails barely seem to grow each month.

How much attention your Pyr will require on a regular basis will vary greatly from dog to dog. If you don't feel you can handle all the chores involved in your Pyr's grooming, consider hiring someone to do it for you. Is there a

A well-groomed, properly nourished Pyr radiates health and well-being.

responsible young person in your neighborhood who would enjoy spending time brushing your dog? Will your dog walker or pet sitter clip your dog's nails once a month? Can you take your Pyr to the grooming shop every few months for a bath? There are solutions to every problem. Just make sure you don't skimp on the quality of your Pyr's care.

Brushing

It takes most experienced owners about 30 minutes to brush out a Pyr's coat. If your Pyr loves to run through the woods and pick up burrs and brambles, or roll in a nice dirt patch, your brushing time could be longer and more frequent.

✔ To brush your double-coated Pyr, begin by using a good-quality, sturdy, wire dog brush or a wire slicker brush that has bristles slightly bent at the ends.

✔ Put your Pyr in a *stand-stay* (see Stand-Stay, page 75). Start your grooming at the dog's head and work your way to its tail, being sure to brush its neck, front legs, shoulders, chest, belly, back, sides, hips, rear legs, and the plume of its tail. (A puppy may not like brushings at first, but it will soon grow to look forward to this weekly ritual.)

✔ While brushing, look for any bumps or lumps under the surface of the skin or any areas of sensitivity. One advantage to frequent brushing is that you will spot potential problems.

✔ If, while brushing, you discover a mat, it is probably easiest to use a dematting comb to get rid of it. This specialized comb has blade edges between the teeth that shave through the mat to loosen it up. It causes less pain than trying to comb through a mat and is relatively simple to use.

During shedding season (spring), brushing your Pyr will be a daily job. Your dog will shed so much hair you may begin wondering where it is all coming from and when the ordeal will ever end. During this time, it is helpful to have a wide, long-toothed steel comb to help remove or strip dead hair.

Brushing your Pyr's coat on a regular basis isn't all you'll need to do.

Eyes and ears: To keep your dog healthy, you'll want to wipe its eyes clean with a damp cotton ball. Your dog's ears should be wiped with a dry cotton ball to remove waxy deposits and dirt.

Nails: At least once a month, you will need to clip your dog's toenails. Though you will be able to use a medium-size dog nail clipper to trim a puppy's toenails, in order to trim an adult's toenails you will need to use a sharp, sturdy, giant-size toenail clipper. To smooth ragged edges, you might also choose to grind them down using an electric grooming tool designed for this purpose. The nail grinder can also be used to trim nails.

Dental care: Bad breath is not a normal condition for Pyrs. Granted, a dog's breath generally does not smell minty fresh, but if your dog has a particularly offensive odor, it's probably related to tooth decay or gum disease.

There are many ways to help keep your dog's teeth in good condition. One way is to feed only dry kibble and provide your Pyr with plenty of chew toys. Another way is to brush your dog's teeth. Consult with your veterinarian on the best way to keep your dog's teeth and gums healthy.

TIP

Bathing

When bathing your Pyr, use shampoo designed for dogs. Human shampoos have a different pH level and can irritate your dog's skin.

If you are bathing inside, make sure you close the door to the bathroom to prevent a sudsy-wet Pyr from running through your home. Keep a stack of clean towels ready to dry off your dog after its bath.

Wash your dog's bedding and blankets before washing your dog. You'll want a nice, clean area for your dog to lie on after its bath. There's nothing worse than washing a dog, only to have it lie on a smelly dog bed.

Bathing Your Pyr

Bathing an extra-large dog is a big job. Fortunately, with a Pyr, this is not a task you will have to perform very often—*as long as you brush your dog on a regular basis*. As incredible as it may seem, your Pyr's coat is relatively simple to keep clean if it has the correct Pyrenees coat—a long, course outer coat and a wooly, dense undercoat. In a correct coat, mud and dirt will literally fall out once the coat dries. A good brushing completes the task. There are some Pyrs, however, that do not have a correct coat. These coats, similar to a Samoyed's, will not repel dirt in the same manner and will require frequent washings.

So how often do you have to bathe your Pyr? Some owners who brush regularly only bathe their dogs once or twice a year. Other owners, whose dogs work during the week as guardian dogs and then are brought in on weekends as the family pet and perhaps show dog, are bathed as often as once a week. How often you bathe your Pyr is really up to you and the demands of your lifestyle.

Pyrs can be bathed outside in warm weather or in an indoor bathtub equipped with a nonskid rubber mat and a handheld shower spray. Bathing a Pyr is no different from bathing any other dog, except that you must be sure to thoroughly rinse the shampoo from the dog's coat, paying particular attention to the undercoat. Rinsing the dog until the water runs free of soap bubbles is a good idea—then rinse the dog again.

Nutrition

You can't cut corners when feeding a Pyr. Cheap, poor-quality food will not make your Pyr's coat gleam or your puppy grow up healthy. Make the investment to feed your dog good-quality food. It does not have to be the most expensive food on the shelf, but it should be a food that meets your dog's nutritional requirements and is both palatable and easily digestible. In other words, the food should be manufactured by a pet food company that has done its research and uses quality ingredients.

Types of Food

There are three types of prepared foods you can feed your Pyr: Dry, semimoist, and canned.

Dry foods are convenient to store, and are helpful in keeping tartar levels down. However, these foods have a relatively short shelf life, so be sure to check the manufacturer's date on the package. Dry foods can also have a high level of preservatives, so read the label. Additionally, some studies suggest that feeding dry food may be one of several factors related to bloat. If you feed dry food, be sure to break it up into several meals during the day and provide clean water at all times to avoid gorging.

Semimoist foods are chewy and contain up to 40 percent moisture. The food is palatable (dogs like it), however, it contains preservatives and some dogs have problems forming firm stools with this food. Shelf life is approximately nine months, so be sure to check the manufacturer's "sell by" date, and don't feed the food if it smells rancid, even if the date has not expired.

Canned dog foods have a long shelf life—up to several years. This food is good for dogs with a high risk of bloat, since it contains as much as 80 percent water. It also contains the least amount of preservatives of the three types of manufactured dog food. Canned foods, however, can be costly to feed an extra-large dog, such as the Pyr. Also, this food does not help to cut down the tartar level on your dog's teeth.

Homemade Meals

Of course, you can always prepare your dog's meals yourself, but if you want to create a nutritionally sound diet in your own kitchen for your dog, be sure to consult with a veterinarian in developing an appropriate canine diet. Creating a *balanced* diet at home can be extremely difficult, not to mention time-consuming, but

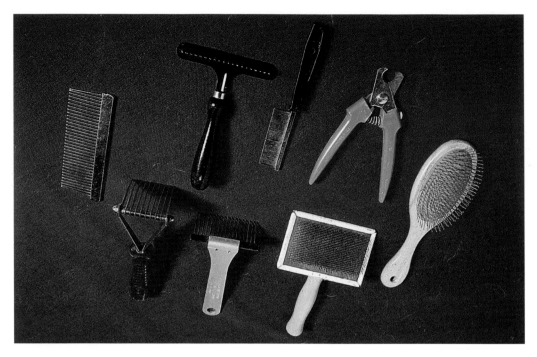

Some of the basic tools you'll need to keep your Pyr looking and feeling its best.

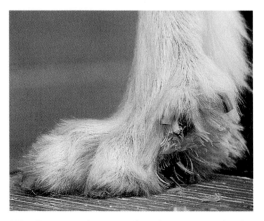

The Pyrenees has two dewclaws on each of its hind legs.

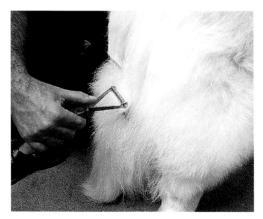

This tool reaches through both layers of the Pyr's double coat to help remove mats in the undercoat.

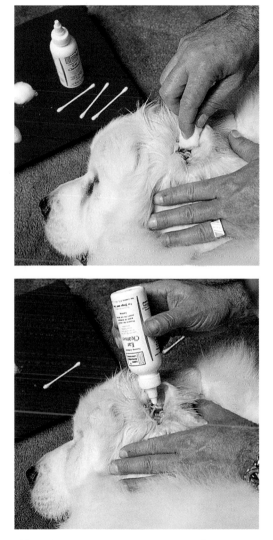

A good brushing once a week should be all it takes to keep your pet Pyr's coat in good shape.

Cleaning ears may require a simple swipe with a clean cotton ball, or a more expensive ear washing with specially prepared products. Be sure to ask your veterinarian how much cleaning your dog requires and how to clean its ears properly.

To help keep your dog fit, make sure to feed on a regular schedule and to use a quality food from a reputable manufacturer.

it can be one of the best ways to meet your dog's particular nutritional needs while avoiding any harmful preservatives. Two references you might want to consult in preparing a natural diet for your dog are: *The Holistic Guide for a Healthy Dog,* by Wendy Volhard and Kerry Brown, D.V.M. (New York: Howell Book House, 1995) and *It's for the Animals Cookbook,* by Helen McKinnon (Clinton: CSA, Inc., 1995).

Feeding the Growing Puppy

What to feed: Because the Pyr is a such a large breed, the puppy grows very quickly and reaches its full height by the time it is one year old. In dogs with a predisposition for developing hip dysplasia, this rapid growth is thought to possibly initiate the onset of the disease (see page 67 for more information on hip dysplasia). For these reasons, many breeders and veterinarians recommend that a Pyr puppy should not be fed puppy food past six months, at which time it should be switched over to a quality adult dog food. Supplements are also not recommended for growing puppies.

The exact cause of hip dysplasia continues to be an area of great speculation and ongoing research; therefore, it is a good idea to consult your veterinarian on feeding recommendations based on the most up-to-date research available.

It is also important not to feed your puppy within an hour before or after very strenuous exercise, to help prevent bloating (see pages 65–66 for more information on bloat), and to always keep fresh, cool water available.

How often to feed: Two to three feedings a day (morning, noon, and evening) are generally sufficient for a young puppy.

How much to feed: It is important not to overfeed your puppy while it is growing. Extra weight will contribute to any potential musculoskeletal problems the puppy might have; therefore, be cautious with free feeding, in which food is left out at all times. If you have a problem keeping your puppy a little on the lanky side, go back to controlled feeding, picking up any food that remains after 15 to 20 minutes.

High-quality dog foods come in various flavors and textures. From left: semimoist, canned, and dry.

Feeding the Adult Pyr

What to feed: A high-quality dog food is a good starting point. Dogs don't get bored eating the same foods over and over again. In fact, if your dog turns up its nose at the food you've been feeding, chances are either the food is stale and doesn't taste good (a fresh bag will solve this) or your dog is ill. If you do choose to switch foods, do so gradually over a period of 10 days to avoid any intestinal distress.

How much to feed: With a dog that has as thick a coat as the Pyr does, determining whether your dog is slightly obese or underweight cannot be done simply by looking at the dog; however, if you work your fingers into the fur along the dog's sides, you can get a good feel for how well covered your dog's ribs are. If you can easily feel the dog's ribs, it is too thin. If you can feel the dog's ribs when you exert light pressure on the skin, your Pyr is probably about right. If you can't find your dog's ribs, your Pyr needs to reduce. If you are in doubt, be sure to ask your veterinarian how much your Pyr should weigh.

When to feed: To help minimize your dog's chances of suffering from bloat, break your Pyr's food into at least two smaller meals a day, picking up any leftovers after 15 to 20 minutes. Make sure that feeding times are not within one hour before or after any strenuous exercise.

The Importance of Water

Free access to fresh, clean water is very important to the health of your dog. If a bowl of water is out for your dog at all times, it isn't likely to dehydrate on warm days or to drink huge amounts of liquids at a time. A good idea is to keep a large nontipping bowl in an area to which the Pyr has constant access. The water should be changed daily or after each meal.

Exercise

One of the joys of owning a Pyr as a house pet is its moderate activity level. Once your Pyr has passed the puppy stage, which can last two to three years, it will not need extensive exercise. A nice daily walk and some quality time in the backyard should be all that is necessary to keep your Pyr fit and happy.

IN SICKNESS AND IN HEALTH

A little bit of preventive health care can go a long way toward providing your Great Pyrenees with a healthy, happy life. Many canine illnesses and conditions can be avoided if you take the time and effort to give your dog proper care and regular veterinary attention. Good veterinary care will also help slow the effects of many hereditary or irreversible diseases.

Common Infectious Diseases

The following are some common infectious diseases against which veterinarians most often recommend vaccinating puppies and adults. Be sure to follow your veterinarian's advice as to when your Pyr should be vaccinated and with what vaccines. The necessity for some vaccinations varies, depending upon the region in which you live.

Parvovirus: This virus is a killer of puppies and elderly dogs, and can also infect adult dogs in their prime with serious consequences. The virus can take one of two forms: the gastrointestinal form that attacks the dog's stom-

Any dog that spends time outdoors must be examined for ticks before coming inside. These tiny parasites cause serious illnesses in dogs and humans.

ach and intestines, or the myocardial form that affects a puppy's heart muscles.

Coronavirus: Another virus that affects unvaccinated puppies and adults, *coronavirus* can cause listlessness, weight loss, diarrhea, vomiting, and excessive thirst. When coupled with a parvovirus infection, the infected puppy's or dog's situation can become dire.

Distemper: This viral disease has been recognized for approximately 200 years and is related to the human measles virus. It can affect the brain of a dog, causing seizures and other neurological problems. Of those animals that contract the disease, up to 80 percent of unvaccinated puppies die; more than 50 percent of unvaccinated adults perish.

Rabies: Rabies is deadly to both animals and humans. Though not a tremendous problem in many areas of the country, it is a major problem if it is your unvaccinated dog that is bitten. Don't take this virus lightly: Vaccinate your dog.

Bordetella or kennel cough: *Bordetella bronchiseptica* is a bacterium that causes a persistent and potentially dangerous respiratory infection. The parainfluenza viruses also cause pulmonary problems. The disease is treatable, but recovery is a long, slow process. If you plan on traveling extensively with your dog, attending obedience classes with other dogs, or boarding your Pyr from time to time, your veterinarian may recommend vaccinating your dog against these diseases. (Most boarding kennels require you to show proof of recent vaccination before they will take your dog.)

Canine hepatitis: This form of hepatitis is not transferable to humans; however, it can cause severe liver damage or even kill your puppy or adult dog. There is a vaccine for this disease that is routinely administered to puppies along with vaccines for distemper, parvovirus, and coronavirus.

Regional Diseases

In addition, there may be other bacterial or viral diseases that are regional in nature. Leptospirosis and Lyme disease are two such examples. However, they are swiftly becoming nationwide problems. Be sure to consult your veterinarian if there are any other diseases against which your dog should be vaccinated. And, if you are traveling to another region or a foreign country, be sure that your dog receives the appropriate vaccinations to protect it from diseases in that area, which may differ greatly from the diseases in yours. Determine well ahead of time what vaccinations and quarantine periods are required by other countries and states.

Parasites—Inside and Out

Parasites that feed on dogs can be seasonal and regional. The following are some of the most common parasites that can wreak havoc with your dog's health—and sometimes yours as well. Be sure to ask your veterinarian about parasites that are a problem in your area and how to ward off or treat an infestation.

Worms

There are five common forms of worms that feed on dogs: roundworms, tapeworms, hookworms, whipworms, and heartworms. Roundworms are common in puppies and are transmitted via eggs in the feces. To become infected with tapeworms, a dog must ingest an intermediate host, such as an infected flea, rodent, or rabbit. Hookworms can be transmitted through feces contaminated with eggs and through penetration of the skin by the hookworm larvae. Puppies can become infected by drinking an infected mother's milk. Whipworms maintain their life cycle through fecal contamination. All these worm infections are treatable.

Guard against these nasty parasites: from left, roundworm egg, whipworm, hookworm head and mouth.

Life cycle of the heartworm, which can be fatal to dogs.

Note: Roundworms, tapeworms, and hookworms can infect children and adults with some rather nasty complications. Make sure when worming a puppy or adult—or even on daily pickup chores—to always wash your hands thoroughly. Also, get your children in the habit of washing their hands before eating and after playing with the dog.

Heartworms are spread by infected mosquitoes carrying infective larvae that are ready to develop into adult worms. The mature worms migrate into the puppy's or dog's pulmonary arteries, where they rest and begin to reproduce. The results of all this are horrible for the dog.

Heartworm can be treated, and in many cases quite successfully. However, there are also many dogs that do not survive the treatment or are so heavily infested with the worm that treatment is impossible. It is easy to prevent heartworm infestations with a daily or monthly pill. Ask your veterinarian how old a puppy must be to begin heartworm preventive care.

Fleas

Spotting a flea on a Pyr can be difficult, and for that reason you may not want to wait until you find one to take action in warding off these annoying, disease-spreading, blood-sucking parasites. Fleas are notoriously difficult to eradicate and are quite resilient. If you live in a warm or moist climate that tends to perpetu-

ate the flea cycle, you may need to have a serious talk with your veterinarian on how to prevent these critters from overtaking your dog, your home, and your life. There are several flea adulticides available that are applied either orally or topically. In addition, there are shampoos, dips, powders, combs, and other less invasive products that may also do the trick for you. Talk with your veterinarian about the best approach in your area.

Ticks

In some areas of the country, ticks are a year-round problem; in other areas, they are a pesky, seasonal parasite. Ticks can carry dangerous diseases, such as Lyme disease, Rocky Mountain spotted fever, babesiosis, and ehrlichiosis. If ticks are a problem in your area, you have to be vigilant with your long-coated Pyr.

Fortunately, there are products on the market that can help keep your Pyr from attracting ticks. These products include dips, insecticidal

collars, and a drop formula that coats your dog's body surface with a chemical that repels ticks. Be sure to ask your veterinarian about the need for a tick preventive program in your area, and determine the best plan of treatment.

Mites

There are five common forms of mites that can cause your Pyr some problems.

1. Chyletiella mites live on the skin's surface and are the cause of what is commonly referred to as walking dandruff.

2. Demodex mites live in the hair follicles and sebaceous glands and are bad news. Their presence causes a red, hairless condition called demodectic or red mange.

A healthy Pyr is a happy Pyr.

3. Scabies mites burrow under the skin to lay their eggs—a condition that is very itchy—causing sarcoptic mange.

4. Mite larvae, or chiggers can be picked up by your dog while romping in the woods or playing in areas of thick vegetation. The larvae's saliva causes swelling and itchiness that last long after the larvae are gone.

5. Ear mites cause the infected dog to produce copious amounts of gritty, dark earwax and afflict it with unbearably itchy and sometimes painful ears.

For each type of mite, there is a specific medication or course of action that your vet-

erinarian may use to eradicate the little pests. If you suspect a form of mite is bothering your dog, get it to the veterinarian's office without delay.

The working Pyr often doubles as the family pet, although it sometimes needs a bath before it lies down in front of the hearth.

Diseases Affecting Pyrs

Bloat: The medical term for this condition is Gastric Dilation-Volvulus Syndrome or GDV. Whatever name you give it, bloat can kill. GDV, though not common in the Pyrenees, is something you as an owner of a large dog should be aware of.

With GDV, the dog's stomach becomes distended or bloated with swallowed air and the stomach twists so that nothing can flow from it into the small intestine. This twisting, in turn, affects the small intestine and the supplying blood vessels. Within a few hours, GDV can bring an otherwise healthy Pyr to the point of death. If the dog receives immediate veterinary care, its chances for survival are better.

The cause(s) of GDV are not well understood; therefore, preventive treatment is not as effective as it is hoped to someday be. What is known is that bloat can kill young and old dogs alike. There is evidence that risk factors could include the type of dog food consumed (dry), the manner in which the food was consumed (in great quantity, at a different time than normal, or with copious amounts of water along with food), and the general temperament of the dog (fearful, stressful).

The current recommendation to try to avoid a bout with bloat is to break up your Pyr's feeding into two or three small meals spaced evenly throughout the day. Keeping a fresh supply of water available to your Pyr at all times will help to prevent it from gorging on water, too. It is also advisable not to feed within an hour before or after vigorous exercise.

Heatstroke: Because the Pyrenees is a heavily coated dog, it is susceptible to heatstroke. Shaving its coat does *not* help this breed handle heat any better; in fact, it may worsen the dog's ability to insulate itself from the heat. To help prevent heatstroke, keep a fresh, cool supply of water available to your dog or puppy at all times. Also, provide your dog with a cool, shady spot outdoors and the ability to come indoors to stay cool. On particularly hot days, limit your dog's activities.

Cancer: Cancer is the biggest killer of older Pyrs (eight years and up) and can even crop up in middle-aged (three- to six-year-old) dogs. The type of cancer that is most common among younger Pyrs is bone cancer. There is no cure for bone cancer with currently available medical technology and therapeutic drugs.

Skin problems: Of the 1,700-plus dogs on the GPCA's health database, the most common problem cited among dog owners was skin problems. Great Pyrenees can have allergies that result in skin eruptions or other problems. Pyrs can be allergic to fleas—in some cases, extremely so.

In many cases, the allergies themselves cannot be avoided, but prompt and regular care of the Pyr's skin under the supervision of a veterinarian (perhaps even an allergist) will help to ease the symptoms. With a flea allergy, the attending veterinarian may prescribe a topical adulticide that prevents fleas from biting the dog.

Ear infections: Ear infections are often a result of allergies. They can also be the result of a foreign body that finds its way into the dog's ear canal. Most ear infections affect the dog's outer ear, similar to a swimmer's ear infection in a human. With an outer ear infection, a dog will often scratch its ears, shake its head, or show signs of pain. The ear may appear inflamed and usually there is a foul-smelling discharge. Outer ear infections are commonly treated by thoroughly cleaning the ear of all wax and debris and then applying topical medicines. An untreated outer ear infection or chronic outer ear infection can lead to middle and inner ear infections, which are much more serious.

Hot spots: The Pyrenees has a double coat (long, outer coat hairs and a soft, downy undercoat) and therefore is more susceptible to hot spots, or areas of acute, moist dermatitis. A hot spot is typically an area of skin that the dog has scratched, licked, or chewed into a circular spot that is moist, inflamed, oozing, and devoid of hair. Once a hot spot gets going, it can quickly double or triple in size within 24 hours. Untreated hot spots can develop secondary bacterial infections, too. Hot spots are frequently found on rear legs, hips, the sides of the dog's torso, and even its face.

To eliminate hot spots, veterinarians first treat the cause of the hot spot (infections, fleas, mites, allergies). The area is shaved, cleaned, disinfected with hydrogen peroxide or iodine, and then a topical anti-inflammatory spray is often prescribed.

Hip dysplasia: A crippling, degenerative disease, hip dysplasia can become so painful that euthanasia is necessary. If you are purchasing a puppy, make sure both parents have received X ray certification that they are free of the disease from a recognized registry (Orthopedic Foundation for Animals, PennHip, or the Institute for Genetic Disease Control in Animals). The current theory is that a trim weight during growth and adulthood, and regular exercise to strengthen muscles supporting the joints may help to prevent or slow the onset of the disease.

Arthritis: If your Pyr lives into its older years (10 to 12), it will get arthritis. This disease often slows an older dog down and causes its joints to stiffen. With most dogs, the onset of arthritis is gradual, but it can also be crippling. Unfortunately, there is no known means to halt the disease or reverse the damage once it's done. There are, however, several things that can be done to make an affected dog more comfortable, such as limiting forceful exercise, maintaining a healthy weight, and permitting the dog plenty of rest.

Consult your veterinarian for additional effective treatments.

Patellar luxation: With this condition, the patella, or the canine equivalent of a kneecap, moves out of place, causing either a temporary altering of the dog's gait or persistent lameness. It is the second most common orthopedic problem among Great Pyrenees. Surgery is often necessary in serious cases.

Paneosteitis: This disease causes lameness, typically in young dogs between five and fourteen months. The pain may last only one or two months, or it may rotate from leg to leg for up to a year. Fortunately, this disease is self-limiting and seems to go away on its own.

Osteochondrites dissecans (OCD): Young dogs may suffer from OCD, a disorder affecting the shoulder, elbow, hip, stifle, or sometimes the vertebrae in the neck. OCD is a degenerative condition in which sections of cartilage are exposed to the joint. Inflammation can be severe and painful. Surgery is sometimes needed.

Dwarfism: Fortunately, this condition is relatively rare and usually can be spotted by an experienced Pyr breeder or owner while the affected dog is still a young puppy. A dwarf Pyr develops into a stunted-looking dog. It is thought that dwarf Pyrs may have congenital problems linked with the gene controlling the dwarfism.

In general, the well-bred Great Pyrenees is a healthy breed with relatively few health problems. This wonderful characteristic of the breed should not be taken for granted, however, and owners should provide their Pyrs with regular veterinary care and be informed on potential health problems.

If these sweet, cuddly puppies are trained early and consistently, they will be excellent companions like this adult. Once you've taught your Pyr the essentials, you can branch out into specialized training for sports such as competitive or just-for-fun Agility or Carting. Pyrs can also be trained for community service, like this visitor to a local nursing home.

The Basics

Because the Pyr is a very big dog, most owners are helpless if their Pyr becomes suddenly ill, hurt, or otherwise immobile. For that very reason, it is extremely important that Pyr owners plan for the unexpected and be prepared to take the measures necessary to get their dog to veterinary help as quickly as possible. A Pyr owner might even consider the services of a house call or mobile veterinarian.

✔ Keep the phone number of your veterinarian and 24-hour emergency clinic in a handy place.

✔ Keep a complete copy of your Pyr's veterinary records. If you need to go to a different veterinarian (for instance, at the 24-hour clinic), it is a great help for the veterinarian to be able to reference the dog's medical history.

✔ Know how much your Pyrenees weighs. Because of its immense coat, most people **overestimate** the body weight of a Pyrenees by 30 to 35 pounds (13.6 to 16 kg). This overestimation can cause a fatal error in emergency anesthetics and therapeutic drug treatments.

✔ Maintain a list of all medications your dog has taken. Document the reasons and the dates and keep this information in an easily accessible location.

✔ Ask your veterinarian about emetics and antidotes in case your Pyr ingests a poison. Keep the substances and directions for their use in an accessible location.

✔ Set aside a thick, sturdy blanket that can be used in a pinch as a stretcher for your Pyr.

✔ Keep rags and old T-shirts that can be torn to construct a makeshift muzzle (which might be necessary if you try to move a Pyr in great pain).

✔ Know which neighbors you can call upon in an emergency to help you carry your injured Pyr to the car. Keep their numbers on your refrigerator.

Basic First Aid

Read up on basic first aid measures regarding bleeding, fractures, snake bites, heatstroke, and other potential problems or injuries. Your veterinarian should have some information to hand out to you. Other sources for information include: *Rescuing Rover: A First Aid and Disaster Guide for Dog Owners*, by Sebastian Heath, Andrea O'Shea, and Karen Cornell (West Lafayette, Indiana: Purdue University Press, 1998) and *Help! The Quick Guide to*

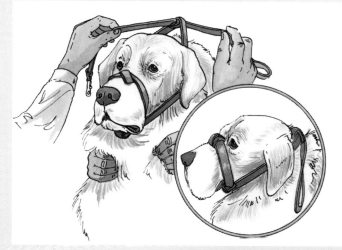

Have someone steady the Pyr as you attach an emergency muzzle.

First Aid for Your Dog, by Michelle Bamberger, D.V.M. (New York: Howell Book House, 1993).

On the Way

With an injured or gravely ill animal, time is usually critical. Do not waste it! Load your Pyr as quickly as possible, tell your veterinarian you're on the way, and describe the problem as concisely as possible. If someone else is present, you can save valuable time by having that person call the veterinarian while you get the Pyr in your vehicle.

If Your Pyr Can't Move

If your Pyr cannot get up, you probably will not be able to lift it up. Take the blanket you've reserved as a stretcher and lay it behind your Pyr. With the help of at least one other person, roll your Pyr over and onto the blanket. Lift the ends of the blanket and carry the dog to the car.

How to Make a Muzzle from Rags

When a dog is in pain, a muzzle is often needed to prevent the dog from lashing out.

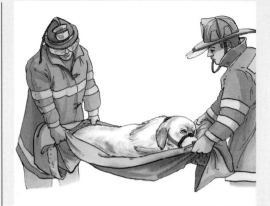

It takes two strong people to transport an injured adult Pyr.

Even the sweetest Pyr may bite if it is in great pain, so don't take a chance. Take a long strip of rags, or anything similar, and loop the strip around the dog's muzzle, crossing under its jaw. Pull both ends behind the dog's ears and tie securely. If done correctly, the dog should be able to breathe easily, but will not be able to open its jaws to snap.

BASIC TRAINING

The Great Pyrenees must begin its training as a young puppy if you are to have a controllable, well-mannered pet as an adult.

Why Train Early?

The reasons for training you Great Pyrenees are twofold: As a breed, Pyrenees grow very rapidly and become large and potentially uncontrollable at an early age. An eight-week old puppy is the size of a small, adult Beagle. At four months, a male Pyr puppy may weigh as much as a Labrador Retriever. A growing, untrained puppy can wreak havoc in an owner's life.

The second reason early training is important is that the Pyr is a natural guard dog, and its innate tendencies must be molded into behavior acceptable to today's society. To do otherwise and allow a Pyrenees to grow up untrained and unruly would be negligent on the owner's part and might result in a tremendous liability on a leash.

Finding a Training School

Yes, if you are an experienced trainer, you could train your Pyr without ever attending a group class or a training school. However, most

The well-trained Pyr is an ideal companion.

trainers take their young charges to group training classes for the simple reason that they can expose their dogs-in-training to a variety of situations.

Puppy Kindergarten

For beginners and experienced trainers, the best way to train your Pyr is to enroll in a puppy kindergarten class. In this class, you will work on the basic commands (*sit, stay, come, down*), and on socializing your puppy with dogs and people. You will benefit from working with an experienced trainer and your puppy will benefit socially from working in a group. You will also quickly realize that your puppy's problems are not as severe as they may seem and that many other owners are having the same problems with their puppies. You'll get some great practical advice on how to housebreak your puppy, survive the teething stage, discourage barking and jumping, and many other situations that almost all puppy owners experience.

Before you sign up with a puppy kindergarten class, however, be sure to screen the training organization carefully—not everyone trains in the same manner. Ask your veterinarian and the breeder you bought your pup from (if the breeder is in your area) which school he or she recommends. Other sources for good recommendations are friends and neighbors with well-trained dogs.

When you visit the training school, the instructors should be pleasant and eager to answer your questions. You should feel very comfortable with the instructors and the way they teach owners to teach their dogs. If you see the instructors encouraging owners to use a heavy hand with the pups or rough handling in any way, run—don't walk—out the door.

If the school makes any guarantees that your pup will be trained by a certain date to perform certain commands, you have a right to be suspicious. In training, there are two variables: your training ability and your dog's trainability. No one can make a guarantee when these factors can range so widely.

In general, if you work with your puppy every day on the training tips that are taught each week in class, you and your dog should progress steadily through the basic and intermediate levels of training. If you are dedicated to your dog's training, you will have a much better-behaved dog than one that is untrained. You will also find yourself enjoying your dog's company more and more.

The following are some of the essential training elements you will learn in a puppy kindergarten class, as well as a few training tips for everyday situations.

Good Behavior

Leash Training

One of the first things you will want your young puppy to do is to learn to walk on a leash. Your puppy must learn that when it hits the end of the leash, it must stop and it must not attempt to drag you around the block. In order to accomplish this, you should start working with your puppy immediately.

✔ With the puppy's collar on, attach a sturdy, six-foot (1.8-m) leash. Do not use a leash that allows the dog to run back and forth at will. Though these retractable leashes may spare you a few pulls in the early stages, your puppy will never learn that it must stop before it hits the end of the leash.

✔ With the leash and puppy attached, begin the pup's leash training by walking around your backyard. Your goal is to keep the puppy near your side. To do this, you will need to keep its attention on you. Praise, treats, and clickers can be used to gain your pup's attention.

✔ If your puppy begins to forge ahead, and your voice, treats, or clickers cannot get its attention, then a little tug on the leash to get the pup's attention is appropriate. Praise the dog when it pays attention to you. Do not praise the pup when it ignores you.

✔ Be *very* careful with your "attention" tug. It should not be hard enough to yank the puppy around, nor should it be so soft that the puppy does not notice your tug.

Sit

The old school of training used to have owners pull up slightly on their dog's collar while pushing down on the dog's rump to put it into a *sit*. This method may work well with a small, weak dog, but with a Great Pyrenees that has a rather strong rear end, this method can quickly turn into a battle of wills and end in frustration.

The new school of training uses treats to entice the puppy to sit. With a stomach the size of a Pyr puppy's, tidbits can be a great motivator. In the new *sit* method, the owner holds the pup's collar with his or her left hand. With a treat in the right hand, the owner says *"Sit,"* slowly passes the treat by the dog's nose, and holds it close to and over the dog's head. The pup's natural reaction is to sit back to get the treat. It sounds tremendously simplistic, but it really works!

After repeating this exercise several times for several days, your Pyr should begin sitting on command. Eventually, you will not need to give your pup a treat *every* time it sits, though you will want to reward it after its training sessions.

When should you tell your puppy to sit? When you are on walks and want someone to pet your dog, a *sit* is a good way to prevent your puppy from jumping in excitement. When you are preparing meals for your dog, a *sit* will keep your pup from knocking the bowl from your hands and onto the floor. And, of course, when you come home from work, an exuberant Pyrenees that has been digging all day in the mud that will go on a *sit-stay* is a great way to lower your dry-cleaning bills.

Down

Another handy command is the *down*. Make sure not to confuse your dog with commands. When telling your Great Pyrenees to remove itself from your couch, be sure to say *"Off,"* not *"Down."*

To teach your dog to lie down on command, put your dog in a *sit*. Then, holding the treat in the right hand and holding onto the dog's collar with the left hand, tell your dog *"Down"* while slowly dropping your right hand to the ground directly in front of the dog. As your dog follows the treat to the ground, it will naturally lie down.

Again, practice makes perfect. Work with your dog several times daily for short periods of time. You'll find your Pyrenees eagerly following commands in a short amount of time.

Stand-Stay

The principles of the *stand-stay, sit-stay,* and *down-stay* are very similar. The simplest to teach, at first, may be the *stand-stay*. It is definitely useful for visits to the veterinarian and groomer, and in the show ring.

To teach your Pyr to stay in the standing position, try the following technique. While your dog is standing at your left side, hold the leash with your left hand close to the dog's collar, pulling up just enough to "feel" the dog. Then, with your right hand, hold your hand in front of its nose and say firmly: *"Stay."* (The reverse use of hands may also be used.) Begin walking counterclockwise around your dog while holding the leash, praising the dog softly as long as it stands still. When you return to your starting point, the dog at your left side, you may release the pup with an "O.K." and praise it lavishly.

Once your Great Pyrenees is performing a *stand-stay* at this level, you will want to increase its proficiency by putting it on a *stand-stay* and then walking away from it a couple of paces, *keeping the dog on leash.* When you hit the end of the leash, turn around and repeat the *stay* command. After a pause, return to the dog. Once you've released the dog from the command with an "O.K.," you can praise lavishly and reward with a treat.

To advance to the *sit-stay* and *down-stay,* the same technique works. Put the dog in the *sit-stay* or *down-stay,* walk to the end of the leash, repeat the command (for reinforcement),

A sit-stay can keep a muddy set of paws on the ground and off you.

The Recall

This command can be a lifesaver for dogs of all ages. In puppy kindergarten or beginning group classes with puppies, the *recall* is often taught as part of a play exercise. The puppies are allowed to play with each other in a small ring. One by one, the owners are asked to call out their puppy from the play group. They are encouraged to do **whatever it takes** to get their puppy out of the play group—whistle, call, clap their hands, get on all fours—anything goes. Once the puppy comes out, it is immediately rewarded with lavish praise and a treat, and then allowed to go back into the play group. In this group setting, the puppy is always rewarded for coming when called.

and then return to the dog. Eventually, you will be able to drop the reinforcement and increase your distances and times away but in sight of the dog. Use a recall leash for these greater distances.

Advanced obedience work can include hand signals that can be used at increasingly greater distances and off leash.

Carting is a sport for the Pyrenees to which the breed and its owners have taken quite a fancy.

The greatest deterrent to a recall, however, is when an owner calls and calls a puppy and gets so angry at the little pup for not coming that he or she punishes the puppy when it *does* come. Not good. Would you want to come to someone who punished you? Make sure that at all times you reward your Pyr for coming.

Family Fun

Another approach to the *recall* exercise with young pups is to do the family recall. In this exercise, family members sit apart from each other and take turns calling and rewarding the puppy when it comes.

Once your pup has progressed in its training to learn the sit-stay, you can use the longer recall leash, walk a few paces away, and give the command "*Come*," along with a tug on the leash. Encourage your dog to come as fast as it can. When it comes to you, reward it. (Later, you can add another *sit* in front of you and a *heel* command to put the dog back in its *heel* position.)

When your Pyr does obey the *come* command on a regular basis, don't tempt fate and try to show off your dog's new skills in an open area or one filled with potential temptations. Continue to reinforce the *come* command in controlled situations. Then, if you ever have to use the command in an emergency, your Pyr should be well conditioned to respond correctly.

Discouraging Barking

The number one complaint of Pyrenees owners—and most likely their neighbors—is that the Great Pyrenees barks, a lot. Again, this is simply a quality of being a good guard dog that doesn't quite fit into the standards of today's society, or in some homes. Added to the barking irritability factor is that the Pyr does most of its barking at night.

Now, before you panic, not *all* Pyrenees are big barkers. Within the breed there is a range, but even a quiet Pyrenees still *barks*. The good news is there are some training techniques available to you to help lessen the barking your Pyr does.

✔ First, try to reduce your dog's exposure to stimuli. If your dog is outside most of the time, perhaps it is time to bring it indoors. Inside the confines of your home, your dog will hear and see fewer things that might make it bark. And, if it does bark, it won't be under your neighbor's bedroom window.

✔ If your Pyr continues to bark on a frequent basis while inside, you can try to teach bark-control training. The goal of this training is to reward your Pyr for a one-woof alert bark and *not reward* extensive barking. In other words, your dog is rewarded for speaking up in appropriate situations only.

✔ The next time your dog begins barking, say "*Shhhh*," "*Quiet!*," or some other command it can easily recognize, and then put the dog in a *down-stay*. (Dogs are less likely to bark when they are lying down.) Immediately reward its quiet behavior.

Collar Controls

If this training method fails and you have a habitual barker that is about to drive you wild, you might consider one of the collar controls available on the market. These collars react when the dog barks. For example, one collar sprays the dog on the underside of its jaw with a liquid such as water or citronella when a barking vibration is detected. Another collar delivers a slight electric jolt every time the dog barks. And a third collar, which is frequently used on retrievers being trained for field events, is a collar that delivers a shock at the control of the owner.

It is important to be aware that if the collars are used without close supervision by the owner, they will not be as effective. Pyrenees have a high tolerance for pain and may simply disregard the inconvenience of the spray or the pain of the electric shock in order to continue barking. With the manually controlled collar, there is a greater chance of accidentally abusing the Pyr. So, before embarking on a collar program to quiet your Pyr, be sure to ask the advice of your veterinarian, breeder, or a trusted professional trainer. You may need a combination of techniques to get the desired response from your Pyr.

Practice Makes a Better Dog

As with all training, positive reinforcement, consistency in commands, and frequent but brief training sessions are the most effective. Patience is a must with Pyrs, as is a firm and consistent hand. Remember, once you hurt your pup's feelings, it may be difficult to recover its enthusiasm. And slow does not mean stupid; your Pyr may perform at a relaxed pace, but don't worry and don't laugh and hug it when it plops down to rest in the middle of a training session, as comical as that may be. Reinforce only the behavior you want. As long as it does what you want it to do,

Dealing with Aggressive Behavior

To help train your Great Pyrenees to ignore, or at least not provoke, other dogs while out on a walk, the following are some tips recommended by Pyr breeders and owners.

✔ *Always* walk your dog in a controlled manner on a leash.

✔ Avoid allowing your Pyr to "run out" on a retractable leash in crowded areas.

✔ Make sure your Pyr is well trained and responds immediately to basic commands before you walk through a busy area with many people and dogs.

✔ Remain calm when walking your dog. If you're afraid your dog might act up, your Pyr will sense your nervousness and its guarding instincts will only be further aroused.

✔ If your Pyr begins to growl at another dog, give your dog the *sit* command. The object is to regain its attention. When you have regained your Pyr's attention, and it is not growling, you may continue on, preferably in a *heel* (the command for walking *at your side*), so that the Pyr continues to pay attention to you.

✔ Do not praise your Pyr for any aggressive behavior.

when and where you want it to, you have achieved what many dog owners only wish for—a well-trained dog.

ACTIVITIES FOR YOU AND YOUR PYR

Depending on the natural abilities of your Pyr, and your abilities as a trainer, you may find that you and your dog can compete or participate in a variety of competitive and noncompetitive events.

The following are brief summaries of the various activities in which you may wish to participate with your Pyr. Because these events require physical exertion or a certain degree of physical maturity, it is wise to have your veterinarian affirm that your Pyr is physically capable of beginning training.

The Sporting Life

Conformation

In order to show your dog successfully in the show ring, there are a few prerequisites. First of all, and most important, you must own a drop-dead-gorgeous Pyr with nearly faultless conformation, great movement, and a good, stable temperament.

In addition, you must learn to be a competent handler who can show off a dog while, at the same time, personally being unobtrusive. And finally, you must be able to train your dog to go through the judge's paces and stand very still for examination.

A Pyr flies through the tire jump in Agility competition.

If you have a pup with potential, and are interested in the show ring life, enroll in a handling class for you and your puppy. In the class, you will be taught how to gait your dog (trot smoothly around the ring with a group of dogs and in a straight line for the judge), stack your dog (set it in a *stand-stay* with its legs, head, and tail in the proper position), and groom your dog to perfection.

To earn a championship, your dog will need to accumulate 15 points under at least two different judges, including at least two majors, which are shows in which there are *lots* of Pyrs.

For more information on rules and regulations for competing in the conformation ring, contact the American Kennel Club, 5580 Centerview Drive, Raleigh, North Carolina 27606; 919-233-3600; "Getting Started" information: http://www.akc.org/showing.htm.

Other helpful resources are the books *Dog Showing for Beginners*, by Lynn Hall (New York: Howell Book House, 1994) and *Show Me! A Dog Showing Primer*, by D. Caroline Coile (Hauppauge: Barron's Educational Series, 1997).

Obedience

In an obedience trial, it doesn't matter what your Pyr looks like or how well it gaits; what *does* matter is how well it performs the various required exercises. At the Companion Dog (CD) level, you and your Pyr will be required to adequately show that your dog can *heel* and *sit* both on and off lead. Also, you and your dog will have to perform a *recall* exercise, a long *sit,* long *down,* and *stand* for examination.

Three passing scores are required for a dog to earn its CD title. If you find you enjoy obedience training, you may want to further your dog's learning and work toward a CDX (Companion Dog Excellent), and perhaps, eventually, a UD (Utility Dog) title, or even an OTCH (Obedience Trial Champion).

For more information regarding obedience or for a local training center, contact the AKC's obedience department (see page 84).

Canine Good Citizen

If you're not quite so competitive, but would like some sort of title to show how well trained your dog is, you might be interested in participating in an AKC's Canine Good Citizen test. It is a pass/fail program that involves ten tests of your dog's ability to be a good canine citizen with both strangers and strange dogs. A passing score earns you and your dog a certificate.

Your local training center should have information and classes available to prepare you and your dog for this test. You can also contact the AKC for a copy of the test rules and a free information kit by writing the AKC, Attn: CGC (see page 84) or call the Canine Good Citizen Program Department at 919-854-0175 or 919-854-0176; General information: http://www.akc.org/cgc.htm.

Dancing with Dogs

If you and your dog have done well in obedience, but are looking for something a little more offbeat, then musical canine freestyle might be for you. In this developing sport, the dog and owner perform a choreographed routine to music while in costume. There are divisions for on-lead and off-lead routines as well as single dog and handler and multidog and handler performances. Contacts in the sport include:

Canine Freestyle Federation, Joan Tennille, 4207 Minton Drive, Fairfax, Virginia 22032.

Musical Canine Sports International, Inc., Sharon Tutt, 16665 Parkview Place, Surrey, B.C., Canada V4N 1Y8; 604-581-3641.

Patie Ventre (Heinz-sponsored canine freestyle events), P.O. Box 350122, Brooklyn, New York 11235; 718-332-8336.

Agility

If you enjoy obedience trials but are looking for a little more flash and excitement—without dressing in costume and dancing with your dog—you might enjoy Agility. Much like stadium jumping for horses, Agility involves a race against the clock through an obstacle course. A well-trained, enthusiastic Pyr will have a great time with this event, as will its owner. Note, however, that because of the amount of exertion required for this event, Pyr owners may want to avoid competing during the hottest summer months.

Many obedience clubs also train for Agility events and are a good starting place for any Pyr owner interested in getting involved in this exciting sport. Other contacts include:

Agility Association of Canada, 638 Wonderland Road South, London, Ontario N6K 1L8, Canada.

American Kennel Club, Obedience Department (see page 84).

North American Dog Agility Council, Inc., HCR 2, Box 277, St. Maries, Idaho 83861.

United Kennel Club, 100 East Kilgore Road, Kalamazoo, Michigan 49001-5598

Helpful books are *Enjoying Dog Agility: From Backyard to Competition,* by Julie Daniels

(Wilsonville, Oregon: Doral Publishing, 1991) and *Agility Training: The Fun Sport for All Dogs*, by Jane Simmons-Moake (New York: Howell Book House, 1992).

Tracking

Pyrs have excellent scenting abilities. With the right attitude and a training regime that begins at an early age, a Great Pyrenees could do well in scent work.

The AKC offers three levels of testing in Tracking, all of which are noncompetitive and are scored as pass/fail:

1. The first level, Tracking Dog (TD), requires a dog to track a scent through turns and various elevations and find the scent article at the end of the trail.

2. The second level, Tracking Dog Excellent (TDX), is more difficult and involves an older scent, a longer trail, and a variety of obstacles.

3. The most recent addition to the Tracking field, Variable Surface Tracking (VST), includes a trail that is laid over field and man-made surfaces. A dog that earns all three titles will receive a Tracking championship.

For more information, contact the AKC, Performance Events (see page 84).

Noncompetitive Activities

Animal-Assisted Therapy

For a dog to be good at animal-assisted therapy, it must have a calm, even temperament. If its ears are accidentally pulled, its paw mistakenly stepped on, or its fur gripped a little too tightly, the dog must be tolerant. Many adult Pyrs have the potential to become outstanding therapy dogs. Their flashy coloring is a visual stimulant to patients, the Pyr's lush, thick coat provides a tactile experience, and the low excitability of most Pyrs make them great therapy dogs.

For certification, many programs require both owner and dog to undergo a training program that culminates with a test. In some areas, this certification program is not available. If this is the case in your area, check with your local dog training club to find out who works with or trains therapy dogs and handlers in the area.

Resources: The Delta Society, one of the largest national animal-assisted therapy organizations, can direct you to the program and training site nearest you. A home study kit is also available along with a myriad of brochures, pamphlets, articles, and other materials related to animal-assisted therapy. For more information or a catalog, write or call: The Delta Society, 289 Perimeter Road East, Renton, Washington 98055-1329; 1-800-869-6898, extension 15; Fax 206-235-1076; http://www.deltasociety.com.

Getting Off the Couch

If you've never participated in a sport or activity with your dog other than choosing the toppings for your Friday night pizza, you might be surprised at how much fun dog sports can be. Your Pyr will enjoy being with you and will appreciate the special attention it will receive in your training sessions. As an owner, you will find fellow dog owners and competitors to be quite social and supportive. In addition, you will also discover that as you and your Pyr work toward a common goal, the human-animal bond will deepen and your Pyr will become more treasured as a life partner than ever before.

Great Pyrenees Breed Information

Great Pyrenees Club of America: The GPCA provides prospective Pyr owners with a comprehensive packet of information on the breed, complete with guidelines for the care, feeding, and training of young puppies. To receive a packet, contact the GPCA corresponding secretary through the American Kennel Club's customer service information line (919-233-9767), or electronically by e-mail (info@akc.org), the AKC's breed club information page (http://www.akc.org/bredclub. htm), or the home page of the GPCA (http://www.akc.org/ clubs/gpca/).

Breeder Referral: The GPCA provides a breeder referral service to people interested in purchasing a quality Pyr from a reputable breeder. The current contact for this service can be accessed by contacting the AKC at the above phone number or at the breed club web site. The home page of the GPCA also contains information on breeder referrals.

Breed Rescue: The GPCA's national rescue committee was formed exclusively to help find homes for discarded—but otherwise healthy and lovable—Pyrs. For more information on the program, to make a much-needed donation, or to adopt a Pyr in need, contact GPCA rescue. The current contact for this service can be obtained through the AKC at the above phone number or the rescue web site: http://www. akc.org/rescue.htm. The GPCA

web site also contains national and regional rescue information: http://www.akc.org/clubs/gpca.

American Kennel Club (AKC): The AKC puppy packet can be obtained by writing or calling consumer services: American Kennel Club, 5580 Centerview Drive, Suite 200, Raleigh, North Carolina 27606-3390; 919-233-9780. The AKC maintains an informative web site that not only has breed profiles (Pyr included), but also helpful dog information. It's a good idea to keep the AKC's address and telephone number on file for any registration questions you might have. The general web site, and the location at which information on all of the AKC's performance events can be obtained, is: http://www. akc.org.

Breed-Specific Magazines

The Bulletin: Published bimonthly by the GPCA for club members, this is an informative magazine for all Pyr owners and prospective Pyr owners. The publication covers pertinent health issues, tips on training and grooming, recent show results, as well as a variety of general-interest topics. For subscription information, write: Darryl Goolsbe, Editor, *The Bulletin*, 6405 Brentwood Drive, Ft. Worth, Texas 76112.

Dog Magazines

Dog Fancy
Subscriptions
P.O. Box 53264
Boulder, Colorado 80322-3264
303-666-8504

Dog World
Subscription Department
P.O. Box 56240
Boulder, Colorado 80322-6240
1-800-361-8056

AKC Gazette
5580 Centerview Drive
Raleigh, North Carolina 27606-3390
919-233-9780

Videos

Dogs, Cats and Kids: Learning to Be Safe Around Animals, by Wayne Hunthausen, D.V.M. For ordering information, contact: Pet Love Partnership, LP, Suite 200, 1 East Delaware Place Chicago, Illinois 60611 1-800-784-0979

Sirius Puppy Training Video, by Ian Dunbar, Ph.D., MRCVS. For ordering information, call: Sirius Puppy Training @ 510-658-8588.

Books
Great Pyrenees

Strang, Paul. *The New Complete Great Pyrenees*, New York: Howell Book House, 1991.

Puppy and General Training

Ackerman, Lowell, Gary Landsberg, and Wayne Hunthuasen (Editors). *Dog Behavior and Training: Veterinary Advice for Owners*, Neptune City, New Jersey: TFH, 1996.

Benjamin, Carol Lea. *Mother Knows Best: The Natural Way to Train Your Dog*, New York: Howell Book House, 1985.

_____. *Surviving Your Dog's Adolescence: A Positive Training*

Program, New York: Howell Book House, 1993.

Delmar, Diana. *Help! My Puppy Is Driving Me Crazy*, Pownal, Vermont: Story Communications, 1997.

Dunbar, Ian. *Dr. Dunbar's Good Little Dog Book*, Berkeley, California: James & Kenneth Publishers, 1992.

McLennan, Bardi. *Puppy Care and Training: An Owner's Guide to a Happy Healthy Pet*, New York: Howell Book House, 1996.

Rutherford, Clarice and David H. Neil. *How to Raise a Puppy You Can Live With*, 2nd Edition, Loveland, Colorado: Alpine Publications, 1992.

Wrede, Barbara J. *Civilizing Your Puppy*, 2nd Edition, Hauppauge, New York: Barron's Educational Series, 1997.

Breed Rescue/Adopting the Adult Dog

Benjamin, Carol Lea. *Second Hand Dog: How to Turn Yours into a First-Rate Pet*, New York: Howell Book House, 1994.

Palika, Liz. *Save That Dog: Everything You Need to Know about Adopting a Purebred Rescue Dog*, New York: Macmillan General Reference, 1997.

Papurt, Myrna L. *Saved: A Guide to Success with Your Shelter Dog*, Hauppauge, New York: Barron's Educational Series, 1997.

Walker, Joan Hustace. *Dog Adoption: A Guide to Choosing the Perfect Pre-owned Dog*, Indianapolis, Indiana: ICS Books, 1997.

The Great Pyrenees has a long history of pastoral guarding, and today guards sheep, cattle, horses, and even chickens with a calm and watchful eye.

Miscellaneous

Crolius, Kendall and Anne Montgomery. *Knitting with Dog Hair*, New York: St. Martin's Press, 1994.

Ott, Sandra. *The Circle of Mountains: A Basque Shepherding Community*, Reno, Nevada: University of Nevada Press, 1993.

The Author

Joan Hustace Walker is an award-winning writer specializing in animals, health care, and environmental issues. She is a member of the Dog Writers Association of America, Authors Guild, American Society of Journalists and Authors, and Society of Environmental Journalists. A dog fancier for more than 20 years, Walker's own canines have been nationally ranked in obedience and performance events.

Acknowledgments

This book would not have been possible without the kind assistance of many Great Pyrenees owners and breeders who were willing to share their time, expertise, and love of the breed. In particular, I would like to thank Janet Ingram and Linda Weisser, both "Pyr people" of the highest caliber, for their countless hours of help with this project.

Important Note

This pet owner's guide tells the reader how to buy and care for a Great Pyrenees. The author and the publisher consider it important to point out that the advice given in the book is meant primarily for normally developed puppies from a reputable breeder; that is, dogs of excellent physical health and good temperament.

Anyone who adopts a fully grown Great Pyrenees should be aware that the animal has already formed its basic impressions of human beings. The new owner should watch the dog carefully, including its behavior toward humans, and should meet the previous owner. If the dog comes from a shelter, it may be possible to get some information on the dog's background and peculiarities.

There are dogs that, for whatever reason, behave in an unnatural manner or may even bite. Under no circumstances should a known "biter" or an otherwise ill-tempered dog be adopted or purchased as a pet or show prospect.

Caution is further advised in the association of children with dogs, in meeting with other dogs, and in exercising the Great Pyrenees without a leash.

Even well-behaved and carefully supervised dogs sometimes do damage to someone else's property or cause accidents. It is therefore in the owner's interest to be adequately insured against such eventualities.

Cover Photos

Isabelle Francais: front cover, inside front cover; Pets by Paulette: inside back cover; Donna J. Coss: back cover.

Photo Credits

Duff Munson: pages 8, 69 top; Bonnie Nance: pages 17, 20, 64, 72; Tara Darling: pages 24, 52; Donna Coss: page 33; Toni Tucker: page 37; Isabelle Francais: pages 2–3, 40, 60; Pets by Paulette: page 68 top; C.W. Hustace: page 80; all other photos by Billy Hustace. Photo of painting on page 9 courtesy of William Secord Gallery, New York, NY.

All inquiries should be addressed to:
Barron's Educational Series, Inc.
250 Wireless Boulevard
Hauppauge, NY 11788

http://www.barronseduc.com

Library of Congress Catalog Card No. 99-072420

International Standard Book No. 0-7641-0734-8

Printed in Hong Kong
9 8 7 6 5 4 3

With its luxuriant white coat and its steady gaze, the Great Pyrenees is a large, magnificent animal of breathtaking beauty. The Pyr was originally bred by the Basque people to guard their livestock in the rugged mountains of southwest France. Its size, strength, and courage enabled it to guard its flocks against wolves, bears, and other predators. Today, these qualities make the Pyr a loyal guardian of home and family. Puppies look like toy polar bears—furry, cute, and cuddly. Gentle, consistent training must begin early, because those babies grow. And grow. And eat. And eat. But the investment in time and money a Pyr owner puts into the care and training of this impressive dog will bear major dividends in love, devotion, and companionship.